TEATRICS

d-aCT I's

$$(i)=\Sigma[(1^70)+\{1^{31}3\}]^n=\{\equiv\}$$

**George's Mum was in this position
just like his Dad {She} the b-littled
only daughter of a dour First World
War Survivor and a disapproving
uncontrolled epileptic Mum
(He) the fellow b-littled from
a working class family of eight
He survived the Second World War
He was her out. She pregnant ended
married to her own World War
Survivor iT worked two mirroring
and mirrored survivors until
death did them part**

judgin' Him!'
'Na! Na! I'll be
d-aCT instant reply
ye!'(His) last act 2nd
sittin' there waitin' tae judge
up in Heaven wi' God the Father
besides ye'll soon be joinin' them
been deed for a lang time now an'
lookin' after ye but they've both
wi' both yer Ma and Da still alive
your thinkin' ye're still in childhood
now and ye've lost yer memory an'
George explained 'Well Da yer Auld
still alive?'...(His) final concern
happening?'...'Is my Ma and Da
'Fit's happening Son?'...'Fit's
George visited regularly
Personhood remained intact
his memory for Time and Place
Before he died George's (Dad) lost

$$\{i\}=\Sigma[\{1^7 0\}+(1^{31}3)]^n=(\equiv)$$

d-aCT II's

d-aCT I's

$$\{i\}=\Sigma[(1^31).\{1^604'\}]^n=\{\equiv\}$$

a {br}Other
a miNefuLL
blocked
from
hAViNG
bEiNG it type
{br}Other a tan
traumatized
d-oUTiCRAT
naG chAMPA
incensed
oNE

oNE
incensed
twin sister
traumatized
overs a tan
mum's left
sHARE of their
from hAViNG his
half blocking him
thrift "(m)Other"
d-Act II spend
pair she now the
thiNEfuLL twin
a miNefuLL

$$(i)=\Sigma[(1^31)+\{1^70\}]^n=\{\vdots\vdots\}$$

d-aCT II's

d-aCT II's

$$\{i\}=\Sigma[\{1^70\}+(1^{31}3)]^n=(\equiv)$$

**(Mustafa)'s first had done
as he had expected b-littled
and raged at him. She
delighted in hiS money
She was in clover
Act II beckoned
He's now in clover
He has the kids. She's
back with her Mum**

off the phone
substitute never
own first (m)Other
(m)Other and his very
big sister their demeaning
then with their demeaned
How could he ever cope
Better be no son's
preferring Mum
of a demeaning boy
She the demeaned
to their first a girl
has just given birth
{Tuba) his 2nd

$$\{i\}=\Sigma[\{1^7 0\}^*(1^{31}2)]^n=(\text{≡}$$

d-aCT I's

d-aCT I's

$$\{i\}=\Sigma[(1^70)+\{1^{71}2\}]^n=\{\equiv\}$$

**{Dave}'s demeaning social
circumstances led to him
smoking and dealing in dope
His dole cheque proved
handy when out**

preferring {d}A
of a demeaning Girl
{He} the demeaned
with little Girls
lead him to interfering
His infantile circumstances

$$\{i\}=\Sigma[(1^{7}0)+\{1^{71}2\}]^{n}=\{\equiv\}$$

d-aCT II's

d-aCT I's

$$(i)=\Sigma[(1^70)+\{1^{31}3\}]^n=\{\equiv\}$$

George remenbers well the spare words
of his Grandad after he came to stay
'That's fine {Moll} now you jist ging
awa back doon 'e stairs' upon
placing his said meal before him
b-littling Dads lack and hence
don't do loving word's of
accepting meaningful
approval

from behind
domineeringly
take his next
determined to
his 4th was
(James) after

$$\{i\}=\Sigma[\{1^7 0\}+(1^7 1)]^n=(\boxplus)$$

d-aCT II's

d-aCT I's

$$(i)=\Sigma[\{1^70\}^*(1^{71}2)]^n=(\equiv)$$

{Tuba) the demeaned of a demeaning
boy preferrring Mum as explained
has been seething inside when
breast feeding recently her own
newborn boy-mAN forever on
the phone in the background
being lovingly raged at by
his own b-littling first
(m)Other substitute

not when
since he knows
them from behind
domineerlingly taking
lost count. He has been
big (br)Other has long
{John) (James)'s

$$\{i\}=\Sigma[\{1^7 0\}*(1^7 1)]^n=(\boxplus)$$

d-aCT II's

d-aCT I's

$$(i)=\Sigma[(1^70)+\{1^71\}]^n=\{\equiv\}$$

{Liz} has been passsively domineered
frontwise by her 'nasty' big (Bert}
for over twenty years now
Having just transitioned to
II her first grandchild
little Bertie dare not
look her in the eye

at the time
was showing
He's no idea what
so nasty little buggers
cinema and took out 20 or
popped into his local Rave
picked up his Mum's AK-47
buy new. So what did he do
No fcuking money to fix or
{Nick}'s X-Box blew last week

$$\{i\}=\Sigma[(1^70)+\{1^71\}]^n=\{\boxed{\vcenter{\hbox{::}}}\}$$

d-aCT II's

d-aCT II's

$$(i)=\Sigma[(1^7 1)+\{1^7 0\}]^n=\{▦\}$$

{Pina} was a
dancer a six pack
a day choreographic
dancer rEAL she felt
when inhaling the
self-identifying
movement of
oTHERs on or
off sTAGE

off sTAGE
oTHERs on or
movement of
the {Pina} full
ironically
miRRORing
rEAL he felt when
choreographic dancer
dancer a Dans Theatre
{Jiri} too was a

$$\{i\}=\Sigma[\{1^7 0\}.(1^7 04')]^n=(\equiv)$$

d-aCT III's

d-aCT I's

$$(i)=\Sigma[(1^70)+\{1^{31}3\}]^n=\{\equiv\}$$

{Molly} quietly just worked away
doing the needful cleaning shopping
laundreying and tidying up after her's no
knowledge of loving approval, no kisses or
cuddles on her part her's lacked that. she
the b-littled daughter of a dour First
World War Survivor who hadn't
known and couldn't do
kisses and cuddles

for her then...but
there and had iT aLL
now that he could have been
drunkin' vomit he was wishing
had just drowned in her own
(Joe})'s daughter {Linda)

$$\{i\}=\Sigma(1^70)^*\{1^70\}^*(1^70)^n=(\text{⁝⁝})$$

d-aCT II's

d-aCT I's

$$(i)=\Sigma[\{1^70\}^*(1^{7^1}2)]^n=(\equiv)$$

{Tuba) has had enough
Breast feeding done she is
of a mind now to take out
a restraining order on her
persistent raging phone calls
to him. But she remains stuck
in Act I reluctant to make a move
secure in her role as the boy-Man
desiring (m)Other figure first
Oedipal {turner) that she is
but constantly suspicious of his
own unrivaled love for her given
his constant understanding
acceptance of his first
(m)Other substitute's
lovingly raging calls
Act II is a cert!

their Childhood
had done throughout
just as he and (Mary})
just fend for themselves
the kids well they could
counted for eachOther and
that (Mary}) and (him})
Adulthood he knew for sure
and now finally centred in
known throughout Childhood
did not count iT is all he had
and her Love for him. Kid's
secure in his Love for her
(Joe}) was secure

$$\{i\}=\Sigma[(1^{7}0)^{*}\{1^{7}1\}^{*}(1^{7}0)]^{n}=(\text{⣿})$$

d-aCT II's

d-aCT I's

$$[U]=[1^{31}3]=[\equiv]$$

**Look @ our [Greek]
(br)Other's indebted
State today**

lately Union
[European] come
charged by their
And @ the Interest

$$[U]=[1^{31}3]=[\equiv]$$

d-aCT II's

d-aCT II

$$\{i\}=\Sigma[(1^70)+\{1^{31}3\}]^n=\{\equiv\}$$

{Pyrrho} along
with {Alexander}
horsed it eAST to
India in 324 BC
Upon his return his
buddhaistic d-aCT
II sKEPTiCiSM
descended
& took root
within the
wEST

paiNs
past his
atom-like
swerving
naturally
whilst
physical
mental and
pleasures both
pursued simple
exile fuLLsomely
Athenian Gardened
{Epicurus} in his

$$\{i\}=\Sigma[(1^{7}0)+\{1^{31}2\}]^{n}=\{\text{☷}\}$$

d-aCT III's

d-aCT I's

$$\{i\}=\Sigma[(1^{7}0)+\{1^{3}1\}]^{n}=\{\boxplus\}$$

{Diogenes}'s
cYNiCAL contempt
for ease and pleasure
ostentatiously led
to his living
in a tUB

iT out
simply sat
{zENO} of ciTiUM
fortune and pain
the vicissitudes of
indifferent to
sTOiCALLY

$$\{i\}=\Sigma[(1^70)+\{1^70\}]^n=\{\text{⠿}\}$$

d-aCT I's

d-aCT I's

$$\{i\}=\Sigma[(1^70)+\{1^{31}3\}]^n=\{\equiv\}$$

{Aristotle}
the eMPiRiCiST in
his mETAPHYSiCAL
musings could not
fathom how (Plato)'s
fORMs could both in
form and give rise to
indiviual existants
such as a Horse
a Cow or a
{Plato}

{Wheeler}
a Quark or a
such as a Quasar
sPACE bound iTs
existant tiME and
rise to indiviual
form and give
could both in
infORMATiON
how biTs of
not fathom
musings could
mETAPHYSiCAL
Aristotleian-like
eMPiRiCiST in his
a modern day
{John} Wheeler

$$\{i\} = \Sigma[(1^7 0) + \{1^{31} 3\}]^n = \{\equiv\}$$

d-aCT I's

d-aCT I's

$$\{i\}=\Sigma[\{1^7 0\}^*(1^7 1)]^n=(\vdots\vdots)$$

Four year old
{Mohammed)
had not yet realised
that both he and his Dad
could never ever bE iT
for her his Mum
She having not
yet exposed him
to her lack of
desire for his Dad
Arranged iT was
her coupling
unlike her
conception

conception
unlike his
his coupling
Arranged iT was
for her Mum
lack of desire
exposed her to his
He having not yet
iT for her Dad
never ever bE
her Mum could
that both she and
not yet realised
(Indira} had
Four year old

$$(i) = \Sigma[(1^70)^*\{1^70\}]^n = \{\vdots\vdots\}$$

d-aCT II's

d-aCT II's

$$\{i\}=\Sigma[(1^{7}0)+\{1^{7}0\}]^{n}=\{\vcentcolon\vcentcolon\}$$

{hOMER}
a bLiND
'Look at 'U's
'U's are iT &
'U's have iT
type bARD

type gODDESS
and hE has iT'
hiM hE is iT
'Listen to
dEAFENing
(tHETis) a

$(i) = \Sigma[(1^7 0).\{1^7 04'\}]^n = \{\equiv\}$

d-aCT I's

d-aCT I's

$$\{i\}=\Sigma[(1^404')^*\{1^{31}3\}^*(1^404')]^n=(\textdivision\textdivision)$$

(Kenny}) needed other men
before he could come Threesome's
were his thing He first needed a her
to love a him, a him that would in turn
love such a loving her so that he could
in turn love her too just like him. Boy
he could come then He loving him
first just like her and he loving
her last just like him It's all in
the bracket's. No the head.
Just take a Look

boys and real mEN
mirrorings the stuff of all
him Big man (Kenny}) mirrored
{George)} to love her last just like
by her first just like him and for him boy
then was being invited to be loved too by
{George)}to do the same. Boy {George)}
her before paying then for his old boy
in quick and had his visual way with
(Kenny}) oggled by a stripper nipped
laughs and naked girls it had to be
the town a week past. Drinks
{George)} out for a night on
to re-ignite their past invited
no physical. (Kenny}) keen
an all in the head man
other men years back
been one of (Kenny})'s
{George)} had originally

$$\{i\}=\Sigma[\{1^404'\}^*(1^70)^*\{1^404'\}]^n=\{\mathbf{\Xi}\}$$

d-aCT II's

d-aCT II's

$$(i) = \Sigma[\{1^{31}3\} + (1^{31}3)]^n = (\equiv)$$

Little did the
'oN ne pas
born une feMMe
oN becomes oNE'
bi-eROTiC d-atmoi
moDED *feMMiNiST*
icon SiMONE
(de BEAUVOiR)
know that
she was not
born a bi-eROTiC
d-aTMOi moded
feMMe **but had**
infANTiLEY
become
oNE

aUTREs
white coLOURed
a*UTREs Les eNFERish*
against *Les* fcuking
raged unendingly
into d-aCT II and
transitioned
& mALCOLM
mARTIN
killing of her
(niNA} following the
singing existence
her aLL coLOURs
In the eND of

$$(i)=\Sigma[(1^7 0)^*\{1^7 04'\}]^n=\{\equiv\}$$

d-aCT II Sc I's

d-aCT I's

$$[U]=[1^71]=[\text{☰}]$$

Look @ the time our Lehman [Br]Other's filed for Bankrupcy 1:45 am Monday 15th September 2008 to be precise the first sign of the end of our labouring Global Economic Order our Bankrupt Capitalist Economic Order

ever since....
working Capital
of [Shareholders]
And @ the state

$[U]=[1^71]=[\boxplus]$

d-aCT II's

d-aCT II's

$$\{i\}=\Sigma[\{1^{7}0\}+(1^{71}2)]^{n}=(\text{☰})$$

And think @ how
(Nigsummunu)
the Babylonian
had thought
way back
of keeping
tabs on his
(m)Other's
demeaning
acts by simply
making count
less sad little
marks on
some newly
fired clay
tablet

survival
their drive for
exchanged in
bartered &
aLL tHINGs
Accounting for
counting and
technique for
appropriated his
Captive {br}Others
(Nigsummunu)'s Jewish
And Look @ how

$$[U]=[1^{31}2]=[\equiv]$$

d-aCT II's

d-aCT II's

$$\{i\}=\Sigma[(1^{31}3)+\{1^{31}3\}]^n=\{\equiv\}$$

{Jeff} and {George)}
had been best (m)ates
throughout Medicine. Two
working class lads yet to become
heroes. By the time they met up
at their 10th Medical Reunion
Dinner {Jeff} was settled in
California divorced with two
daughters and a new male LoVer
{Ralph} {George)} was intrigued
He asked tentatively...'So {Jeff} Who?
Who?'...'What do you mean?'...' Who does
the fcuking?...'I do the fcuking'...he blurted
He a b-littled little Big {Jeff} boy man
who didn't have iT did the fcuking
What the fcuk was going on here!
Bugger iT! even more things
to solve. Fcuking Bugger iT!

of all mU (m)ates
mirrorings the stuff
reciprocation Mutual
of {Jeff}'s a mUtual
and in the case
{Jeff@110}
{George@001)}
(Kenny@001})
in (Kenny})'s case
mUtual identification
have taken the form of a
and his {m}ates mirrorings
The stuff of {George)}

$$\{i\}=\Sigma[\{1^404'\}*(1^{31}3)*\{1^404'\}]^n=\{\text{≡}\}$$

d-aCT II's

d-aCT I's

$$(i)=\Sigma[(1^70)+\{1^{71}2\}]^n=\{\equiv\}$$

{Jill} the demeaned
had been demeaned
by a girl sister preferring
Dad Her straggly haired little
girl lost look tends to make her
attractive to protective Big boy
(m)Otherly types There have been
lots The last bought her a house but
stayed still with the wife Things never
change much with {Jill} She go's with
the flow and tidys up
occasionally

miRROR surfaced
months before his miTHER
flown the Communal Nest
on his 1st Birthday and
had married his Sheila
heads though. Tommy
Sheila or Uncle Tommy
mum's words. No Auntie
bugger Uncle Alex one, his
the favourite and a cheeky
Auntie Nettie (one})
Mummy. A straggly haired
some far more pleasing
boy {one)} off pleasing
An often absent Daddy
she could show love
cleaning one, only way
A forever Molly Mummy
fitting Grandma (one})
left it's Trench A persistently
Granda one that had never
to 6 Heads A First World War
Boy George ended up attached

$$\{i\}=\Sigma[\{1^{4}04'\}*(1^{31}3)*\{1^{4}04'\}]^{n}=\{\rlap{=}{\equiv}\}$$

d-aCT II's

d-aCT III's

$$\{i\}=\Sigma[(1^704')^*\{1^70\}^*(1^704')]^n=(\equiv)$$

Shakespeare
the di-eROTiC
d-aCT III
iRONiC
(William})
mAN
was
LoVable
{maBEL)}
tells {m}E

was not
can-er
d-aCT I no
nothing new
no alternative
(Beckett) the

$$\{i\}=\Sigma[\{1^71\}+(1^{31}2)]^n=(\equiv)$$

d-aCT I's

d-aCT I's

$$[U]=[1^4 04']=[\text{☷}]$$

**Look @ the Universal
ways of our Apostolic
[Catholic] [Christian]
{br}Others & sisters
arising from their
approriation and
critique of the Old
Testament ways of
their Abrahamic
Elder [Jewish]
{br}Others**

{br}Others
[Catholic]
of their elder
Testament ways
Worldly non-New
their critique of the
& sisters arising from
[Christian]{br}Others
of our [Presbyterian]
And @ the Bookish ways

$[U]=[1^404']=[\text{☷}]$

d-aCT II's

d-aCT I's

$$\{i\}=\Sigma[(1^71 2)^*\{1^504'\}]^n=\{\Xi\}$$

Twelve year old (Tom}
will have the option in Adult
life of being the stripped naked
male lover of either a female
or male lover given what's inside

his head no his bracket's no his body
a male body attached to a female

and male mummy and daddy
head with only the female

head oggling a male body
no daddy head oggling
a female one. Mirrored
mirrorings the stuff of us all
so when Act I (Tom}'s male
body is dutifully getting
undressed for his active
oggling female lover
his attached male
oggling female head
will be anticipating
not his own but her

pleasure to come

pleasure to come
not her own but his

will be anticipating
oggling female head
male lover his attached male
undressed for his active oggling
(Tom}'s male body is hastily getting
the stuff of us all so when Act II
a female one. Mirrored mirrorings
a male body no daddy head oggling
head with only the female head oggling
a female and male mummy and daddy
no his body a male body attached to
inside his head no his bracket's
or male lover given what's
male lover of either a female
of being the stripped naked
remember in Adult life
will have the option
Twelve year old (Tom}

$$\{i\}=\Sigma[(1^{7}{}^{1}2)^{*}\{1^{5}04'\}]^{n}=\{\Xi\}$$

d-aCT II's

d-aCT II's

$$[U]=[1^71]=[\text{☷}]$$

Look @ all of our
past {br}Others and
sisters put to the sword
by our past and present
Koranic reciting
{br}Others

{br}Others
Abrahamic
[Christian] Elder
their [Jewish] and
Testament ways of
the Old and New
and critique of
approriation
Mohammed's
from The Prophet
and sisters that arise
[Islamic] {br}Others
Biblical Ways of our
And @ the other Ancient

$[U]=[1^4 04']=[\text{☰}]$

d-aCT II's

d-aCT I's

$$\{i\}=\Sigma[(1^{31}3).\{1^{4}04'\}]^{n}=\{\equiv\}$$

Niccolò {Machiavelli}
a cynical Realist of the
Politics of his Florentine
day..no wonder.given
the babbling buzzing
free-play of
mis-matched
Groupings
of any and
every *PoLiS's*
day Groupings
aRiSTiCRATiC
miLiTiCRATiC
tHEOCRATiC
and cRiTiCo
CRATiC aLL
vying for
top dOG

{O}sama bin Laden
{br}Other's pupil
unlike his Saudi based
the Grand Mosque of Mecca
Millennialist seizure of
{br}Other {al-Otabi}'s
ever witnessing his
President Nasser before
sedition by US owned
of d--aCTs II & III for
was hanged on the cusp
Frankfurter critique
Post-Enlightenmet
Adorno and Horkeimer's
vioLENCE no different from
and obsessed with sEX and
individualistic materialistic
which for him was basically
ardent critic of the US
man was in his day an
Muslim {br}Other
a clear thinking
Sayyid (Qutb}

$$\{i\}=\Sigma[(1^{31}3)^*\{1^404'\}]^n=\{\text{☰}\}$$

d-aCT II's

d-aCT I's

$$\{i\}=\Sigma[(1^{31}3).\{1^{4}04'\}]^{n}=\{\equiv\}$$

{Martin} was
a black man
a dignified
cRiTiCRATiC
black man
'that was the
way gOD
made him'
hiS dAD told
him...only his
dAD though
ended up
knowing
why

him
made
dAD had
domineering
favouring
way his un
that was the
his favourites
kids litttle boys
man who loVed
fANTiLE black made
made man a loVing in
too was a black
{Michael}

$$\{i\}=\Sigma[(1^70)+\{1^{31}2\}]^n=\{\text{≡}\}$$

d-aCT II's

d-aCT I's

$$\{i\}=\Sigma[\{1^70\}+(1^{31}3)]^n=(\equiv)$$

(Ricki) double
aspected {Ricki)
an old Trainee of mine
had always intrigued (m)E
He was one of those rarest

of events A 'Look@(m)E
I'm none of them' years later

he was even A 'Look@(m)E
I don't have iT but I am iT'

one His new wife was a
stunner Wow! and he
had flipped from an earlier
presumed pre-Oedipal state of Mind
to an Oedipal one Wow! I didn't think
that was a possibility in Adulthood
then. So onto the streets for a count
of the number of pre-Oedipal
subjects aware of Parental
Desire just like Ricki) who'd

obviously bested his own
rival Daddy substitute
Unlike his Trainer

True!
scary but
Mum Wow!
preferring
{br}Other
ing ways of a
the demean
grounded in
resentiment
infantile
Reverend's
that of the
identical to
resentiment
grounded in infantile
Religious Thing was simply
What if the whole Christian
Presbyterian revelation
{John} an upstanding
Reverend Doctor
to (m)E the
was a revelation
(Buntie})'s {John}

$$\{i\}=\Sigma[(1^{7}12).\{1^{5}04'\}]^{n}=\{\Xi\}$$

d-aCT I's

d-aCT I's

$$[U]=[1^{71}2]]=[\text{≣}]$$

An abRAHAMic
truth grounded in
the accumulated
feelings and
thoughts
of individual
domineered or
d-littled past present
(br)Others passed over each
for some far more favoured
younger (br)Other or sister
that had resulted in
each crossing to
that [L]AWfull
Other shore

{br}Others
all more favoured
cruxifiction of any or
a helpful tool in the literal
unfavouring {f}Other and as
comeback for their own real
purely as a demeaning form of
in the Name of the {F}Other
restricting LAW laid down purely
LAW that Legalistic constraining &
and laid down then the [n]ORAL
{br}Others who'd erected
individual resentful
primed shore of
This [1^{7}04']

[U]=[1^{5}04']]=[Ξ]

d-aCT I's

d-aCT I's

$$\{i\}=\Sigma[(1^{31}3).\{1^{4}04'\}]^{n}=\{\boxminus\}$$

{Christopher}
the trOt railed
brilliantly against
all totalitarian
regimes whether
religious or political
both before and after
the fall of the Berlin
Wall alas the rOt
set in following
his championship
of the ways of
Anglo-American
neo-Darwinian
Capitalist regimes
whilst oblivious to
the last of his very
own mU driven
b-littling
regime

the trOt
{Christopher}
elder {br}Other
far more favoured
the ways of his ungODLy
Christianity and railed against
ways f Anglo-American
d-littling unfavoring
championed the
the unfavored
{Peter}

$$\{i\}=\Sigma[(1^{31}2).\{1^{5}04'\}]^{n}=\{\Xi\}$$

d-aCT I's

d-aCT I's

$$(i) = \Sigma[(1^7 1)^*\{1^6 04'\}]^n = \{\equiv\}$$

(Ariella} and {Arabella)
matched Well almost
domineered both in
childhood (eLLa} by her
Jewish Mum {beLLa) by
her German Dad (eLLa}
wore no mascara {beLLa)
did (eLLa}'s Grandfather
had esaped his {br}Others
didn't they were gassed
and burned {beLLa)'s
Grandfather likewise
didn't escape he had
to do the gassing & the
burning Two matching
LooK @ U Helpex Girls
Grandad products of
double crossed histories
happily now sharing
the same bed unlike
the Grandads

Zionist Contemperories
Teutonic Ancestors and
Other within unlike their
masters of the rejecting
LooK @ U Helpex Girls
escape. Two matching
unaware of his {br}Other's
the Other waited his turn
one gassed & burned as
not do as they were told so
iT hit them. Both daren't
gassing & burning until
had no knowledge of the
Grandfather's {br}Others
Grandfather and (eLLa}'s
(eLLa} didn't need to {beLLa)'s
Jewish Mum {beLLa) wore mascara
by her German Dad (eLLa} by her
domineered in childhood {beLLa)
definately matched both
{Arabella) and (Ariella}

$$(i) = \Sigma[\{1^7 1\}^*(1^6 04')]^n = (\equiv)$$

d-aCT I's

d-aCT I's

$$(i)=\Sigma[(1^{3}{}^{1}3).\{1^{4}04'\}]^{n}=\{\equiv\}$$

**Sick of being seen
and starred as the
"Banality of EviL"
oNE she searched
out in her mind's
eye her ex-fascistic
Lecturing LoVer
from her student
days for some
intellectual
succour**

oNE
Mummy
'zuhanden'
Elfride his
Daddy figure
his vorhanden
exile Hitler
to go into
balls in infancy
not having had the
favoured Hannah
Daddy's little
'vorhanden'
She his

$$\{i\}=\Sigma[\{1^{7}1\}.(1^{6}04')]^{n}=(\equiv)$$

d-aCT I's

d-aCT I's

$$[U]=[1^{31}2]=[\Xi]$$

**Look @ the History
of the Black Power
Movement of our
[Black] American
(br)Others and sisters
that pushed early on for
self imposed exiLe and
segregation from
their disempowering
[White] (br)Others
and sisters**

Color exclusivity
without any in-built
[br]Otherhood of Man
a Socialist plea for the
A critique that ended in
forms of "black racism"
and condemnation of all
And @ their later critique

$[U]=[1^4 04']=[\text{≡}]$

d-aCT II's

d-aCT I's

$$(i)=\Sigma[\{1^{7}0\}+(1^{31}2)]^{n}=(\text{≣})$$

**Think @ how (Beka)
the demeaned of a
demeaning [Israeli]
secular pair must have
felt when accepted by
some recently settled
[Zionist] settler Group
when visiting the West
Bank and how (She)
had b-littlingly rejected
such an unsettling
acceptance**

and sisters
settler {br}Other
Group of [Zionist]
of such an accepting
the West Banking ways
must have unsettled
@ how she in turn
And Think also

$$[U]=[1^{3}1]=[\text{≡}]$$

d-aCT II's

d-aCT I's

$$(i)=\Sigma[\{1^604'\}*(1^71)*\{1^604'\}]^n=\{\equiv\}$$

{Phyllis)} can't avoid being
a stripper given what's inside
her head. She loves iT when they
oggle her first, just like her Dad used
to oggle her Mum and last when they
leave her booth and are oggled by her
fellow strippers, just as her Mum used to
oggle her Dad. It's all in the bracket's.
no the head no the body a female
body attached to a male and
female daddy and mummy
head the male head oggling
the mummy body first and
the female head oggling
the daddy body last
Mirrrored Mirrorings
The stuff of us All

to come
own but his pleasure
anticipating not her
female head will be
attached male oggling
oggling male lover his
undressed for his active
male body is hastily getting
all so when d-Act II (Tom}'s
mirrorings the stuff of us all
oggling a female one. Mirrored
male body no daddy head
the female head oggling a
and daddy head with only
female and male mummy
a male body attached to a
his bracket's no his body
what's inside his head no
male fellow lover given
d-Act II male lover of an
being a stripped naked
can't avoid in later life
Twelve year old (Tom}

$$\{i\}=\Sigma[(1^{7}{}^{1}2)^{*}\{1^{5}04'\}]^{n}=\{\Xi\}$$

d-aCT II's

d-aCT I's

$$(i)=\Sigma[\{1^{31}3\}.(1^{4}04')]^{n}=(\text{☷})$$

(Edna) Euclid
the b-littled and
b-littling oNE couldn't
see the point of any of his
beach sanded drawings
"OK so a Line is a point
gone for a walk then
'EuC' an' two points
are the extremities
of such a Line and
two such Lines are
the extremities
of a Surface and
two such Surfaces
are the extremities
of a Solid. So bloody
what! Go pick and
peel some tomatoes
for tonight's Mousaka
Now that would be
real progress

toPOLOGY
own mU mENTAL
forms structuring his
(m)aLGEBRAiC mUmerical
{d}aLGEBRAiC and
hidden b-littling
oblivious of the
oNE of Euclid totally
within and without the
Topological Spaces both
equations and Geometric
relationships between
thing that study of the
Algebraic Geometry his
mathematical things
forms hidden within all
with the structural forms
'number' or 'size' but rather
mathematical not so much
on fascinated by all things
boy found himself early
b-littled (Grothendieck)'d
Alex a two times

$$\{i\}=\Sigma[\{1^{31}2\}+(1^{31}3)]^n=(\equiv)$$

d-aCT I's

d-aCT II's

$$\{i\}=\Sigma[(1^71)^*\{1^604'\}]^n=\{\equiv\}$$

not mULess
but certainly
clueLess Little
biG Bertie pestered
by the desires of his
biG Little mummy
hEAD inside caved in
recently and had 'her' 38"

Boob job done on the cheap
whilst holidaying in Turkey
languishing now she is on
any bed or beach awaiting
her passive dominance
of any man to come

to come
of any woman
her active dominance
bar or club anticipating
loitering she is now in any
whilst holidaying in Turkey
Boobs removed on the cheap
recently and had her 38"
hEAD inside caved in
her biG Little daddie
by the thoughts of
biG Mabel pestered
clueLess Little
but certainly
not mULess

$$(i)=\Sigma[\{1^71\}+(1^71)]^n=(\stackrel{\scriptstyle\dots}{\dots})$$

d-aCT II's

d-aCT I's

$$\{i\}=\Sigma[(1^31)+\{1^{31}3\}]^n=\{\equiv\}$$

Little
Eugene
having been
Wignered by
his {d}A and
Quantum Physicised
by his Alma (m)ater
managed to symmetrically
quantatize his doubly sPLiT
wORLD upon facing iT
but found nothing
there to do when
facelessly
facing the
other way

other way
faceing the
facelessly
(t)here when
be no longer
(G)weneth to
his true LoVe
lost in finding
but was totally
upon facing iT
Lines and squiggles
in terms of joined up
to everyone's surprise
sPLiT Wignerian wORLD
renormalize his doubly
gifted and managed to
found himself visually
by his Alma (m)ater
Quantum Physicised
by his (m)A and
riCHARDized
having been
Little Feynman

$$\{i\}=\Sigma[\{1^7 0\}.(1^7 04')]^n=(\equiv)$$

d-aCT I's

d-aCT I's

$$\{i\}=\Sigma[\{1^{7}0\}^{*}(1^{7}04')]^{n}=(\equiv)$$

{He) Cronos the product of an
Ancient Greek Affair encouraged
by his mA Gaia had castrated
his dA Uranus and then
married his sister Rhea to
sire umpteen kids males
were swallowed each a feared
castrator just like himself Zeus
his 5th and Rhea's favourite
a bit like my Uncle Jimmie
escaped this Fate
with hER help to
later overthrow
and take over
from hiM yoU
and I being
the End
result

Us aLL
Look on at
and endlessly
but withdraw
oNE had no option
Grand {f}Other
and castrated
the d-LittLed
(Uranus)

$$\{i\}=\Sigma[\{1^70\}+(1^31)]^n=(\overset{\cdot\cdot}{\underset{\cdot\cdot}{=}})$$

d-aCT II's

d-aCT I's

$$\{i\}=\Sigma[\{1^70\}+(1^{31}3)]^n=(\equiv)$$

Think now @ how (Abrahim)'s
(m)Other b-littled and b-littling
Act II Daddy had felt after being
accepted by his revered Jihadist
{br}Others and sister's and how
he must have felt at the height of his
{F}ALLAH inspired flight smashing into
those Towering Symbols of (M)Other
America's b-littling Power annihilating
immediately then 2731 of our American
non-Koranic reciting {br}Others & sisters
and 19 of his Western Trained fellow
reciting {br}Others leaving us all
wondering whether (Abrahim)'s
Grand(m)Other his dAD's
b-littling mUM will
ever Approve

work
good day's
{F}ALLAH's
their b-littling
fallen and praised
had each submissively
{br}Others and sister's
and dusted his Jihadist
deed had been done
how after the
And Think @

$$[U]=[1^{31}3]=[\equiv]$$

d-aCT I's

d-aCT I's

$$[U]=[1^71]=[\boxplus]$$

**Attend and Look @
the Texts describing the
[English] State of Affairs
on Friday 26th June 1314
the day following their
Bannock Burn Defeat
at the hands of their
[Scottish]{br}Others
and sisters**

ever since.....
critique of the [English]
{br}Others and sisters
And @ our [Scottish]

$[U]=[1^404']=[\boxplus]$

d-aCT II's

$$\{i\}=\Sigma[\{1^70\}.(1^704')]^n=(\equiv)$$

He verbally attacked
{m}E outside the Post
Office on the Monday
'Why didn't you go into

partnership with Halldis

and Mike after I retired?'

'James how could I' 'She rushed

into partnership with Mike'
'She totally isolated {m}E'
'Maitland had probably
advised her o' that'

He was floored not the

Gentleman {James} I knew
There was money involved

The Tax man was chasing us
both for extra Tax as a

consequence of his and
and Halldis's actions I had

never been forewarned
of his Retiral.

he jumped

and on the Sunday

following Thursday

It was returned the

and a second for his

one for my own Tax

wrote two cheques

Accountant and

I went into our

on the Thursday

iT I'll show him

my fault was

OK so iT was

$\{i\}=\Sigma[\{1^{31}3\}.(1^{4}04')]^{n}=(\equiv)$

d-aCT I's

d-aCT I's

$$\{i\}=\Sigma[(1^70)+\{1^70\}]^n=\{\text{⁑}\}$$

**{Democritus}'s conclusion
was that he was simply
all aTOMs and vOID**

all forms
rule forms
says nUMBERs
{Pythagorus}'s last

$$\{i\}=\Sigma[(1^{71}2).\{1^{5}04'\}]^{n}=\{\Xi\}$$

d-aCT II's

d-aCT I's

$\{i\}=\Sigma[\{1^70\}.(1^704')]=(\equiv)$

**1st born
(gLAUCON)
the (m)Other
pleasing
favorite**

full fORMs
shADOW
pleasing
of mockingly
inverted theory
with his pay back
(m)Otherly fORMs
the tables on aLL
pleasingly turned
2nd born fORM
unfavored
trumatized
exiled tan
mentally
pleasing
in his un
(pLATO)

$$\{i\}=\Sigma[\{1^31\}.(1^604')]=(\equiv)$$

d-aCT II Sc I's

d-aCT I's

$$[U]=[1^70]=[\vdots\vdots]$$

**Look @ the pre-Simone
de Beauvoir existentially
conventionally submissive
ways of Western
Bourgeoisie
[White]
Girls**

ways
submissive
Critique of such
explicit Feminist
her [Girls] sexually
And @ Simone and

$[U]=[1^{4}04']=[\equiv\!\equiv]$

d-aCT I's

d-aCT I's

$$\{i\}=\Sigma[(1^70)\{1^704'\}]=\{\equiv\}$$

{sHe}
dADDiE's
little girl
his loVing
loVed
d-AcT I
aUNTiE
nETTiE
then

now
LoVer
ex-dA
rejECTED'
Scene II
her d-AcT II
dADDiE oNE he
II disapproving
her d-aCT
{hE}

$(i)=\Sigma[(1^{7}0).\{1^{7}04'\}]=\{\equiv\}$

d-aCT II Sc I's

d-aCT I & II's

$$\{i\}=\Sigma[(1^7 0)+\{1^{71}2\}]^n=\{\equiv\}$$

Think @ how
{Malcolm} not yet
X'd domineered
and demeaned by his
imprisoning circumstances
had felt when released and
accepted by his Black Islamic
Group of segregationist
[br]Others and how
he must have later felt
abandoning them all and
following then his own
ColorLess post-Hajj Path
towards a true [br]Other
hood of man

of mU mankind
hood of the whole
sake of the [br]Other
abandoning them for the
him shot 21 times for simply
abandoned him by having
hood of Islamic [br]Others
his abandoned [br]Other
And Think @ how

$$[U]=[1^71]=[\Xi]$$

d-aCT II's

d-aCT I's

$$\{i\}=\Sigma[(1^70)+\{1^71\}]=\{\boxed{\equiv}\}$$

{Diogenes}
proudly cYNiCAL
got iT He just
lived in a TuB

forms
behavioural
of their bad boy
and cover for both
the fORM of an excuse
His philosophy taking
both carried within
that hE & {Socrates}
of the rejecting Other
purely in the form
was grounded
{Socrates}
of the pleb
that his love
did he know
get iT little
did not quite
favored
the un
(Plato)

$\{i\}=\Sigma[\{1^31\}.(1^604')]=(\equiv)$

d-aCT I's

d-aCT II's

$$\{i\}=\Sigma[(1^70)+\{1^{31}3\}]^n=\{\equiv\}$$

{Aristotle} failed
as well to get iT
no different from
his mentor {Plato}
little did he twig
that his "virtuous"
good boy behaviour
poor little big man
was purely a b-littled
reaction formation
grounded in the
d-littling and
disapproving
circumstances
of his character
forming Infantile

Family Affair

circumstances
all regardless of
indifference to iT
maintaining a Stoic
of Citium involved
Virtue for (Zeno)

$$\{i\}=\Sigma[\{1^7 0\}+(1^7 0)]^n=(\text{⠿})$$

d-aCT II's

d-aCT I's

$$\{i\}=\Sigma[\{1^{7}0/4'\}.(1^{7}0/4')]^{n}=(\text{☰☷})$$

{Abraham}'s (m)A
an' {d}A both fae uR
mESOPATAMia were
polytheists they'd
worship 'onybody'
an' 'a' bloody gOD
like thing nae wonder
{Abraham} and his fellow
tantraumUtised mates
buggered off nomadically
following their sheep
and goats tae CaNAAN

an' erected there their
ancient tabernacle
thiNG tae their oNE

an' only unfavoring
'YaHweW' gOD
that critically
disapproving
rejector of aLL
critically
rejecting
peoples

boY tWiT'ers
disapproving dONNiE
unfavoringly disapproved
a' infantily programmed
the inFANTiLe needs o'
rival's an' opposites
up wantin' the oppositee
rival oTHER an' aye ends
oot the want's o' some

he'd until he susses
eMPTY jist like his
his Bank Account's
a'bODY else's money

rather worships an' uses
disapproved son he
their unfavoringly

aen money nae like
up worshipping a' their
a' their diein' days an' ended
{d}a an' (m)A scrimped an' saved

unfavoringly disapproving
dONNiE boY {truMP}'s

$\{i\}=\Sigma[\{1^70/4'\}.(1^70/4')]^n=(\boxminus)$

d-aCT II's

d-aCT I's

$$\{i\}=\Sigma[\{1^5 04'\}*(1^{71}2)*\{1^5 04'\}]^n=\{\Xi\}$$

Look @ The Book
of Exodus and how
{Moses)} led the
[Israelites] through
the Sinai wilderness to
their post-Egyptian 8th
century BC exiLe via Mount
Sinai where God reveals himself
and offers them the return of CaNAAN
present day Palestine if they made a
Covenant to Keep his Law, the tORAH
A Covenat that really seems
to have worked longterm

chosen People
chosen {F}Other's
tORAH They their
{F}Other's Law the
worship of their chosen
Jerusalem Temple and
and their rebuild of their
Yehud province in 538 BC
approved return to their
exiLe and their Persian
Babylonian Historical
And Look @ their

$[U]=[1^504']=[\Xi]$

d-aCT II's

d-aCT I's

$$\{i\})=\Sigma[\{1^{31}3\}.(1^{4}04')]^{n}=(\text{☷})$$

d-Littled and
b-Littled by iT
aLL drunKeness
(his) post-wAR
adULTescent
response...my
bedroomed to
the right snoring
drunkingly out of iT
Greek God-Like
ex-World
War Jimmie
so'dier Uncle
Jimmied by
his (m)A and
Uncled by his
sister and best
frien' Jim my
{d}A anither
drunkin'
at times
World War
survivor

survivors
Eastern War
each and aLL Middle
(br)Others and sisters
new nATIONed
Ariked by his
and General
his (m)A
Arieled by
so'dier
East wAR
Middle
Jewish
blown
iT aLL full
right above
settling to the
response Our
adULTescent
(hiS) pre-wAR
aLL dominATiON
d and d-b'd by iT

$$\{i\}=\Sigma[(1^71).\{1^604'\}]^n=\{\equiv\}$$

d-aCT I's

d-aCT I's

$$\{mE\}=\Sigma(1^{31}3)^{n}=(\equiv)$$

Lucy
afarensis'
'Zeus-like'
little
{br}Other
Adam the
unweaned
took on and
ousted the
'Uranus-like'
Alpha (m)ale
of their pack in
adULTescence
to sire umpteen
kids with their
sexually
receptive
'Gaia-like'
(m)Other

Others
(f)emale
receptive
sexually
for food &
and forage both
but to go into exile
had no more ado
primate cousins
their ancestral
different from
{br}Others no
weaned elder
Resentfully

$[U]=[1^{31}2]=[≡]$

d-aCT I's

d-aCT II's

$$\{i\}=\Sigma[(1^3 1).\{1^6 04'\}]^n=\{\equiv\}$$

The skandalous
mULTiPLiCiTY
enduréed by
{Bergson}which
lasted clockwise
81 years 4 days 4

mins and 34 seconds
extended into an
in-between the
sheets Influenzal
death having caught

the bug whilst standing
defiantly in d-aCT 04'
line with his fellow

sympathizing and

sympathized Jewish
[br]Others and sisters
awaiting their two-faced
Vichy Governmental
Jewish Registration
despite his own pocketed
Letter of exemption

fall ending
Less free
breath
unfilmed
RépéTiTiON &
in iT's recursive
(DeLEUZE) was
enduréed by
multiplicity
in the skandalous
The diFFéRENCE

$$\{i\}=\Sigma[\{1^{31}3\}.(1^{4}04')]^{n}=(\equiv)$$

d-aCT II's

d-aCT II's

$$\{i\}=\Sigma[(1^70)+\{1^{31}3\}]^n=\{\equiv\}$$

fuLLsome
{Aristotle}
sat on the
edges of his
two valued
this or that
Logical Space
no middle
ground
for him

for him
ground
middle
not no
Space
Logical
or neither
this that both
of his four valued
on the middle ground
lounged peacefully
{nAGARJUNA}
d-emptyfuLL

$$\{i\}=\Sigma[(1^31).\{1^604'\}]^n=\{\equiv\}$$

d-aCT III's

d-aCT II Sc I's

$$\{i\}=\Sigma[(1^{7}0).\{1^{7}04'\}]^{n}=\{\equiv\}$$

He lovingly
laid his little
tiNA in the arms
of some bystander
sat himself down
dowsed himself
in kEROSeNE &
lit the match

A blazing burning
reminder then to
his cHRiSTiAN
nATiON sTATE
of the uncHRiSTiAN
ways of nAPALM
ing oTHERS

Sc I mAJORs
and d-aCT II
d-aCT I miNORs
and miRRORing
aRENA'd miRRORed
egged on by the
driven wars
miNORs mU
d-aCT II
and saVAGE
minded mAJORs
d-aCT I gROUP
barbAROUS
driven wars
world of mU

$$[U]=\Sigma[\{1^7 0's\}+(1^7 04''s)]$$

d-aCT II Sc I's

d-aCT I's

$$(i)=\Sigma[\{1\,^7 1\}^*(1\,^6 04')]^n=(\text{≡})$$

{Blondie) was a Barmaid
a bottled blonde female
Barmaid attached to a male
and female head one of which
oggled the oTHER the male one
in her case. Indeed it was this
female oggling male attached
head that had finally got her
to enhance both her lips and
breasts with silicone purely
for the enhancement of
the pleasure of all oggling
male heads yet to come
Alas it didn't enhance her own
She was indeed oggled more but
frustratingly her attached female
oggling male head still persisted in
being taken up by the coming
of his pleasure rather than her
own confirming the fact
that {Blondie)'s miND is
purely the thought of
her Daddy's bODY

his Mummy's bODY
purely the thought of
that (Carl}'s mIND is
own confirming the fact
her pleasure rather than his
taken up by the coming of
head still persisted in being
attached male oggling female
more but frustratingly his
his own. He was indeed oggled
to come. Alas it didn't enhance
of all oggling female heads yet
the enhancement of the pleasure
with regular routines purely for
finally got him to enhance his Pecs
female attached head that had
indeed it was this male oggling
the female one in his case
of which oggled the oTHER
to a female and male head, one
big muscled Drunk attached
of {Blondie) 's a regular
(Carl} was a regular

$$\{i\}=\Sigma[\{(1^{71}2)^*\{1^504'\}]^n=\{\Xi\}$$

d-aCT I's

d-aCT II's

$$(i)=\Sigma[(1^70)^*\{1^70\}^*(1^70)]^n=(\equiv)$$

Think now @ how our
sweet Princess (Elizabeth})
on her 1953 day had felt when
crowned by the Grace of God
Queen Elizabeth II Queen of the
United Kingdom of Great Britain
& Northern Ireland & other Realms
& Territories Head of the Commonwealth
& Defender of the Faith and accepted
that day into that exalted Group of dead
and dying Kings and Queens of the
United Kingdom of Great Britain
Northern Ireland & other Realms and
Territories Head of the Commonwealth
& Defender of the Faith a glorious
example to Us all that day
of a heavy headed biG little
submissive good little
White Girl

submissive day
White conventionally
had also felt on that gloriously
biG little baD Girl Feminists
Mums of sexually expilicit
the Group of yet to bE
And think @ how

[U]=[1⁴04']=[⬚]

d-aCT I's

d-aCT I's

$$[U]=[1^504']=[\Xi]$$

**Look @ the present
day critical do-iNGs
of that anti-[Gay] Mob**

the Body Politic
of their re-entry into
the passive acceptance
the way for the coming of
exiLed [Gay] Lot preparing
this re-habilitaing post
present day do-ings of
And @ the Legislative

$$[U]=[1^504']=[\Xi]$$

d-aCT I's

d-aCT I's

$$\{i\}=\Sigma[(1^{7}{}^{1}2)^{*}\{1^{5}04'\}]^{n}=\{\equiv\}$$

**Think @ how 22 year
old (Tom} had felt after
stripping naked for his 19th
male lover He a long confirmed
Member with his lack of a
biG member of that Passive
Homoerotic d-aCT II male
Loving Group of past mU
mINORing Ones**

sisterly eVoL
{br}Otherly and
heads are full of Love
fiNGER as long as their
or a woman her middle
where a man sticks his diCK
Politic What does iT matter
their rightful entry into the bODY
{br}Others are presently pushing for
Act II newly turned mINORing
and his backside entering
And Look @ how he

$$[U]=[1^71]=[\overline{\overline{}}]$$

d-aCT II's

d-aCT II's

$$\{i\}=\Sigma[(1^31)+\{1^70\}]^n=\{\vcenter{\hbox{::}}\}$$

{Paul} of Tarsus sin
ified by the Abrahamic
Words of his Saul-ifying
d-LittLing (m)Other
was later graced
on the basis of the
Judeo-sanctioned
sinfully annulling
Crucifixion of
his {F}Other's
one and only
(dis)Approved son
Jesus of Nazareth

There {Paul} stood
converted on the
Road to Damascus

He could do no
other a newly
CHRiSTianized
faithful GOD
approved
mAN

mAN
full GOD approved
CHRiSTianized faith
do no other a newly

yet to come He could

JeWiSH {br}Others
the sake of aLL
{F}Other purely for
forgiving gracefull
Pauline view of a
and championed the
eventually acknowledged
disapproving {f}Other
sON of a mU minoring
He the non-rejecting
side. There he stood
defected to the Roman
fellow revolting {br}Others
suicide of his mU major
following the communal
fender of the JeWiSH Faith
Century no surrender de
{Josephus} the 1st

$$\{i\}=\Sigma[(1^{31}2)+\{1^{7}0\}]^{n}=\{\boxdot\}$$

d-aCT II's

d-aCT I's

$$\{i\}=\Sigma[(1^3 1)+\{1^7 1\}]^n=\{\overline{\overline{}}\}$$

{Bakr} the cloth sales
man sinified by the
ancient Abrahamic
Words of his d-LittLing
Abu-fying (m)Other
fervently sponsered
the prophetic kORANiC
words of his Quraysh
tribal {br}Other
{Mohammed}

There {Abu} stood
converted in his Mi'raj
sanctioned belief of the
heavenly nature of his

Prophet companion on
their Road to Medina

He could do no other
a newly IsLAMified
GOD fearing
mAN

mAN
GOD fearing
IsLAMified
a fully
no other
He could do
and kORAN
by fearfull sWORD
his dead Commander
5 times a day ways of
the GOD sanctioned
(br)Others to
neighbouring
converting all
Commander took to
the death of his Prophet
the Islamic Faith following
surrender defender of
selling Ist Caliph no
{Bakr} the ex-cloth

$$\{i\}=\Sigma[(1^31)+\{1^71\}]^n=\{\boxdot\}$$

d-aCT II's

d-aCT I's

$$[U]=[1^6 04']=[\equiv]$$

**Look @ their bowled hand
their empty begging bowled
hand and their robed yellow
mind-emptied bODY their
own South Eastern
Ways of d-oUTiNG
iT aLL**

iT aLL
Ways of d-oUTiNG
their own Western
downwards singing
roped from the waist
singing their mONKed up
their hooded cloistered
Listen to their singing

$$[U]=[1^{6}04']=[\equiv]$$

d-aCT I's

d-aCT I's

$$\{i\}=\Sigma[(1^31).\{1^604'\}]^n=\{\equiv\}$$

Just out of India
and {Bodhidarma} the yet to be
Patriarched of Zen immediately
rejected his rejecting {f}Other in the form
of the Emperor of China with the words

'No Blessedness only Emptiness'
before sitting down to his
nine year long
emptying stint

'ne. fcukin' traitor
for a fcukin' English tainted
in his Patriarched Glasgae siR-Hood
aboot fcuking {Connelly) throwin'
raving on Sauchiehall Street
Scottish Nat was ranting and
{Joe Brewer} a fervent
Just oot o' the Pub

$$\{i\}=\Sigma[(1^71).\{1^604'\}]^n=\{\equiv\}$$

d-aCT I's

d-aCT II Sc II's

$$\{i\}=\Sigma[\{1^70\}.(1^704')]^n=(\equiv)$$

One cold
Friday
late in
childhood
(Peter) my
Dad's best
fishing
buddy
was left
standing
outside his
Dad's Sawmill
whilst his Dad
went in and
sawed off
his head

help stick iT out
God's as well to
of Moses' Torah and
612 commandments
for they already had the
less bright little buggers
other equally perplexed,
little concern for aLL
like himself but with
bright little buggers
for aLL Perplexed
wrote up his "Guide"
in (d)Adultescence
bugger who later
by him a bright little
{Maimonides} stood
refusing to convert
Arabic conquerers after
of an Infidel's death by his
to Morroco under threat
fleeing from Cordoba
Dad stuck iT out
{Maimonides}'

$$\{i\}=\Sigma[(1^71).\{1^604'\}]^n=\{\equiv\}$$

d-aCT I's

d-aCT I's

$$\{i\}=\Sigma[\ (1\,{}^{7}0)+\{1\,{}^{7}0\}]^{n}=\{\mathbf{\ddot{=}}\}$$

{aL} -'the ProoF of isLAM'
GhAZZALi being the product
of an intolerant common
Medieval Affair taught
that all talk apart from
'Look at yoU (f)ALLAH'
'yoU are iT' and
'yoU have iT'
was incoherent and
superfluous {biN}-LADEN
a similar Modern day
product with his Act II
'Don't Look at Them'
'They're not iT' &
'They don't have iT"

infantile talk and deadly
planes has lately dis-proven
the coherence of aLL such

talk of 'Them' and '(H)im'

for the whole of
mUmankind
and the rest
of tiME

being the end result
objects such as 9/11 Planes
movement and hand built moving
their day The Modern day Materialist
by the Tycho Brahe & Galileo movers of
Christian (br)Others but later dis-proven
approved at first by his neighbouring
and the words of Aristotle words
simply studied the movements of bodys
unmoved neither by dance nor dreams
meditative moments whilst aL 'ProoF' major
the movements of dreamfuLL and whirling
'ProoF' minor took refuge in the study of
moments each re-acted differently aL
outside movements of their wakeful
mOVER both traumatised by the inside &
the gOD of their Day as their unmoved
aL-'ProoF' & (ibN}-aVERROEs-rUSD saw
(H)is wORD occasionally both
In facing and (m)Echoing

$$\{i\}=\Sigma[(1^70)^*\{1^704'\}]^n=(\equiv\}$$

d-aCT II's

d-aCT I's

$$\{i\}=\Sigma[\{1^704'\}^*(1^70)^*\{1^704'\}]^n=\{\equiv\}$$

{Acquinus)}'s
conclusion no
different from
ibN-Avicenna
- (siNA)}'s
showed 'iT'
aLL to bE
grounded
in gOD the
(F)Other

(F)Other
in gOD the
aLL grounded
that 'iT' was
(br)Others was
mATERIALIST
unlike his fellow
conclusion too
(Einstein}'s

$$\{i\}=\Sigma[(1^{3}{}^{1}3)^{*}\{1^{4}04'\}]^{n}=\{\equiv\}$$

d-aCT II's

d-aCT I's

$$\{i\}=\Sigma[\{1^7 1\}+\{1^7 0\}+\{1^{31}2\}$$
$$\{1^3 1\}+\{1^{71}2\}+(1^7 0)]^n=(\text{⠿})$$

a mAN's sON
never knew
him recursive
miNORing
miRRORings
of numerous
{f}Other-like
others and his
side-lined
(m)Other
his lot in
childhood

directions
fantasied
of his long
in the manner
and snuffed out
group miNORed
and a victimized
d-aCT II substitutes
side-lined murderous
substitutes inFANTiLY
of miNORing (m)Other
of a willing young cast
payback in the form
adULTescent
teATRiCAL

$\{1^31\}+\{1^{71}2\}+(1^70)]^n=(\vdots\vdots)$
$\{i\}=\Sigma[\{1^71\}+\{1^70\}+\{1^{31}2\}$

d-aCT II's

d-aCT I's

$$\{i\}=\Sigma[(1^71)+\{1^70\}]^n=\{\text{⚏}\}$$

**Little Tommy bAYES
was confused how
could (sHE) LoVe him
as his God fearing
{d}A reassured
him since she
persisted in
whacking him
6 out of 7 days
most weeks**

bOOLE's concern
not wee Georgie
(sHe) LoVe's mE
(sHe) LoVe's mE

$$\{i\} = \Sigma[\{1^7 1\} + (1^7 0)]^n = (\vdots\vdots)$$

d-aCT I's

d-aCT I's

$[U]=[1\,{}^{5}04']=[\Xi]$

**Look @ their Wars
their Internationally
sanctioned Churchillean
carpet-bombing [L]awful
Wars their way
of demeaningly
domineering
iT aLL**

iT aLL
domineering
way of avoiding and
their draft dodging
a Chance' 60's singing
their doped up 'Give Peace
Google their singing

$$[U]=[1^604']=[\equiv]$$

d-aCT I's

d-aCT II Sc II's

$$\{i\}=\Sigma[(1^70).\{1^704'\}]^n=\{\equiv\}$$

**{He} jumped
an honourable act
rejecting the rejecting
oTHER in-side**

out-side
oTHERs

the rejecting
as (He} blasted
'Allah Akbar' his last

$$\{i\}=\Sigma[(1^7 1)^*\{1^7 04'\}]^n=\{\equiv\}$$

d-aCT II Sc I's

d-aCT II's

$$\{i\}=\Sigma[(1^70).\{1^704'\}]^n=\{\equiv\}$$

{Tommy} Reid
a this side o' the
sod no nonsense
coMMONsensical
sort of bODY thought

& talked like the vulgar
thoughts for him
were as rEAL as the
tHiNGs thought
stones bones
and groans
were as real
to him as his
own (m)A and
{d}A and GOD

'sod aLL non
sensical talk
of imPRESSiONs
and iDEAs iT's aLL
bloody weLL real
real as the biG
buGGER
intended'

percieves iT'
thro'{mE)}
biG bUGGER
the bloody
that bE untiL
odd though
no bloody tree
{d}A 'There's
(m)A to his
just like hiS
the Quod
out there in
talk vulgar
continued to
imPRESSiONs
iDEAs and
LoCKEAN
of secondary
the coming
of the vulgar to
thought and talk
after reducing aLL
Georgie bOY {Berkeley)}

$$\{i\}=\Sigma[\{1^7 04'\}^*\{1^7 0\}^*\{1^7 04'\}]^n=\{\equiv\}$$

d-aCT II's

d-aCT I's

$$[U]=[1^404’]=[\text{☷}]$$

**Look @ their International
Conferences their Academically
based conferences critiqueing
tHiS's and tHaT's tHEIR way
of disapproving
and b-littling
iT aLL**

don't get iT
that 99% Lot who just
domineering that oTHER Lot
their way of avoiding and
obscenely accumulating
Lot that moneyed 1% Lot
Look @ that moneyed

$$[U]=[1^604']=[\equiv]$$

d-aCT I's

d-aCT I's

$$\{i\}=\Sigma[(1^{31}3)^*\{1^404'\}]^n=\{\equiv\}$$

(Fran}ces
....ca WooD
maN a frame
less canvas of
fleeting impressions
uncanvased by her a
series of thought-prints
before (sHe} jumped

as (sHe} jumped
fleeting impression
a canvasless
thought-prints
full series of
(sHe} a face

$\{i\}=\Sigma[(1^{3}1 3)^*\{1^{4}04'\}]^n=\{\equiv\}$

d-aCT II Sc II's

d-aCT II's

$$\{i\}=\Sigma[(1^{31}3).\{1^{4}04'\}]^{n}=\{\equiv\}$$

{Martin} the Adultescent
religiously d-littled (Luther)
a non-indulgent d-littlingly
b-littling {in}tolerant
{d}Adultescent man
made Protestant
[H]istory by further
championing the
Grace-fully
{ }tolerant Ways
of his {F}Other
and Paul's as well
It's all in the brackets
no the Apostles
[T]here he stood
nailing his 95 Theses
to the door he could
do no other a truely
gOD forGiving man

gOD fearing men
{d}ARiA [sh]ARiA bound
each and aLL (m)ARiA
followers they can do no other
just like (h)iSiS modern day
adulterous (m)Adultescents
(t)here he stood stoning
the brackets no the Koran
mystical ones It's aLL in
{aL} GhAZZALi's far more
than the ProoF of isLAM
Muhammad's rather
{F}Other and the Prophet
domineering Words of his
by championing the fearfully
made 18th century Saudi History
b-littling (m)Adultescent man
a non-indulgent d-littlingly
(ibN)'abd-aL-waHAB
(Muhammad)

$$\{i\}=\Sigma[\{1^71\}+(1^31)]^n=(\overline{\overline{}})$$

d-aCT II's

d-aCT I's

$$[U]=[1^{3}13]=[\equiv]$$

Look now @ our past
b-littled and colonised
Central African {br}Others
and sisters presently being
re-colonised and indoctrinated
with that Koran carrying LoT's
{F}Other's sanctioned ways
of disapproving and
b-littling Us aLL

to get iT
who are not meant
99% connable Lot
that oTHER Lot that
avoiding and domineering
accumulating their way of
moneyed 1% Lot obscenely
that moneyed Lot, the
And then again @

$$[U]=[1^604']=[\equiv]$$

d-aCT I's

d-aCT I's

$$\{i\}=\Sigma[\{1^31\}^*(1^604')]^n=(\underline{\underline{\equiv}})$$

Three have birthed
for him so far. He having
left childhood attached
to 6 heads. His 1st was a
d-Act I teacherly {m@101)
demeaning One. He a d-Act I
d-oUTiCRATic (m@011}) One
His 2nd a d-Act I needy (m@111}
disapproving One. He a d-Act I
lovingly (m@001}) b-littling
One. She left and returned
a d-Act II contrite rejecting
0/4' One. Reminded of her
rejection. She hung herself
His 3rd is a d-Act I caringly
(m@111}) disapproving One
He a lovingly d-ActII {m@001)}
b-littled and b-littling One. She
left and returned. Contrite?
No Way! Her d-Act II oNE
is presently divorcing
his b-littled and
b-littling oNE

divorce Exit
for the moneyed
rather make straight
double turners they
re-awakened rejecting
unrealised by out-rivaled or
by guilted suicide. An option
such a rejecting Other within
sometimes a total rejection of
to old rejected oNEs and
{L}Others new or returns
Other within, searchs for
awakening of the rejecting
though typically leads to a re
with d-aCT II attractive substitutes
Daddy substitutes, any involvement
secure always in the unrivaled love of d-Act I
out-rivaled self deception unlike his 2nd
turner condemned to a life of (m@111})
whilst his 3rd was a double (m@111})
his 2nd was a single (m@111} turner
in this ($\equiv$) position different though
His 2nd and 3rd were both

$$(i)=\Sigma[(1^704')^*\{1^70\}^*(1^704')]^n=(\equiv)$$

d-aCT II's

d-aCT I's

$$\{i\}=\Sigma[\{1^704'\}^*(1^70)^*\{1^704'\}]^n=\{\equiv\}$$

{Descartes)} didn't think
near enough. He couldn't. Out
decieved by both surviving Grandparents
in their love for each oTHER unable to think
things through to another end He had no other
option but park himself alongside his now no
longer concieved decieving gRAND{f}Other
in the form of his loving past decieving
grand(m)Other and persistently do
his bidding. His 'Cogito ergo
sum' comforter his
'I think therefore I am'
U'res grand {Daddy)}
comforter happily saw
him through to his
self-decieving End

of them
being only two
aspected {Spinoza}
(Spinoza) the double
number of modes
could take on a finite
mATTER each attribute
were miND and extended
of attributes two of which
with an infinite number
{Diva} ve (Natura)
One substance
Only One

little faith and took off
by the Rabbi's of their demeaning
by both he got himself excommunicated
never ever then bE decieved b-littled
been decieved by either he could
though not have iT Never having
bE iT for both. Only bE iT
aspected {Spinoza} could
(Spinoza) the double

$$\{i\}=\Sigma[(1^{3}{}^{1}3)+\{1^{3}{}^{1}3\}]^{n}=\{\equiv\}$$

d-aCT II's

d-aCT I's

$$[U]=[1^604']=[\equiv]$$

**Take a Look @ the Disabled
and unEmployed outsiders of
present day Social Democratic
Europe and their Chinese
Worker subsidised Dole
cheques and the domineering
and b-littling ways that they
are delt with by the 1%'s
Right Wing Political
Representatives**

don't get iT
connable Lot who just
that austerity packaged 99%
domineering that oTHER Lot
their way of avoiding and
Lot obscenely accumulating
Winged Lot that moneyed 1%
Look now @ that moneyed Right

$[U]=[1^604']=[\equiv]$

d-aCT I's

d-aCT I's

$$\{i\}=\Sigma[\{1^7 0\}+(1^7 1)]^n=(\boxplus)$$

**Occasionally
the (br)Others
Malebranche
{Nicolas} et (Pierre)
happened upon
Things that pleased
both Parents. Boy
did that feel
different!**

(H)is Way
the order of
Repetition being
Difference and
organize iT aLL
recreate and re
skandalously
of iT aLL to
Creator
continuous
the causually
the (F)Other
for God
occasion
a splendid
moment is
passing
that each
the thought
happened upon
full of the pair
more thought
{Nicolas} the

$$\{i\}=\Sigma[(1^7 1).\{1^6 04'\}]^n=\{\equiv\}$$

d-aCT II's

d-aCT I's

$$[U]=[1^604']=[\equiv]$$

Take a Look as well
@ the unacknowledged
state of the ill, the Disabled
and the unEmployed of present
day Democratic America and their
Chinese Worker subsidised Goods
with neither Medical Cover, Dole
Cheque nor money to buy. The
domineering and b-littling ways of
the 1%'s Right Wing Adam Smithed
Political Representatives have
made damned sure of that
there being no alternative.
Adam said so!

get iT
not meant to
who are simply
99% connable Lot
that austerity packaged
domineering that oTHER Lot
their way of avoiding and
obscenely accumulating
that moneyed 1% Lot
Right Winged moneyed Lot
Look @ that Adam Smithed
And a further passing

[U]=[1⁶04']=[≡]

d-aCT I's

d-aCT I's

$$\{i\}=\Sigma[\{1^31\}^*(1^604')]^n=\{\equiv\})$$

mis-matched
they were hE a
d-aCT I (m@011}
b-littling and d-littling
oNe sHe a d-Act I teacherly
{m@101) demeaning One
stuck in d-aCT I hE abandoned
hER and sHe later divorced hiM
mismatched they were
mismatched mirrors
of caLAMiTY

kids
divorcee's
of most
sadly the fate
mUmetic di-pOLEs
mummy end of their
cope with the demeaning
abandoned his kids unable to
disapproving oNE hE later
d-aCT II with a (m@111}
transitioned into
After having

$$\{i\}=\Sigma[\{1^31\}*(1^604')]^n=(\equiv)$$

d-aCT II's

d-aCT I's

$$\{i\}=\Sigma[(1^70).\{1^704'\}]^n=\{\equiv\}$$

{Leibniz}'s conclusion
was that he was not
all nULL and vOID but
simply some mUnified
rational mONADic activity
harmoniously unified with
aLL oTHERs through the
mUnifying rational
mONADic activity of
his and {Spinoza}'s
nATURA-some
(F)Other

oNEs
relativised
mONADically
from {Leibniz}'s
fORMs no different
sPACED bODILY
aLL absolutely
nUMBERs rule
oNE was that
{Newton}'s

$$\{i\}=\Sigma[(1^{71}2).\{1^504'\}]^n=\{\Xi\}$$

d-aCT II's

d-aCT I's

$$\{i\}=\Sigma[(1^71).\{1^604'\}]^n=\{\equiv\}$$

{Thomas}
a rational man
of his Enlightened
times did not get
that iT was the
inFANTILE nasty
brutish and shortish acts
of his Sovereign (M)Other
rather than those of his {F}Other
that had Hobbled him for Life
to the thought of Kings and their
Divine Right to wage War against
subjects whether their own or
those of some other
Divine Right'd King

Nature
state of
(M/F}Otherly
on Life within a
and shortish take
his nasty brutish
alternative given
There being no other
Deaths did them part
their Citizenry until
Absolute Power over
would have to assume
Groupings that necessarily
in all modern Parliamentary
elected (F)Otherly Sovereign with
the case for a constitutionally
turning he did champion
However in his Act II

$$\{i\}=\Sigma[(1^71).\{1^604'\}]^n=\{\equiv\}$$

d-aCT II's

d-aCT II's

$[U]=[1^704']=[\equiv]$

**The nORTH won
beating those
sOUTHERN
mentally
enslaved
enslaving
(m)Other
fcUKERs**

fcUKERs
(m)Other
enslaving
factory
nORTHERN
Lost to those
The sOUTH lost

$$[U]=[1^704']=[\equiv]$$

d-aCT II's

d-aCT II's

$$[U]=[1^{31}2]=[\text{☷}]$$

**2014 was a good
year for the ziONiSTs
they took out 2,100
of those eNCLAVED
pALESTiNiAN
(m)Other
fcUKERs**

eNCLAVERs
fcUKing ziONiST
their (m)Other
take out 72 of
only managed to
on the other hand
pALESTiNiANs
The gAZA

$[U]=[1^{31}2]=[\text{☰}]$

d-aCT I's

d-aCT I's

$$\{i\}=\Sigma[(1^{7}0).\{1^{7}04'\}]^{n}=\{\equiv\}$$

Hutcheson {FH}
a Commonsensical
Scottish Sentimentalist
having lost 6 of his own
to (m)Other Nature divided
iT aLL in {d}AULTescence
inner and outer sense
being populated by the
Commonsensical tHiNGs
o' his Commonsensical
(br)Others inner by his
own commentorial 'MoraL'
Judgements grounded in the
good and bad feelings common
to aLL men upon the some
time tastefully beautiful
and tasteless right and
wrongs o' the tHiNGs
& ways o' his (br)Other
man and (M)Other
nATURE this side
o' the sod

o' the wATER
(br)Others his side
cONGRESSiONAL
bound sLAVE owning
rights bound & arms
of his unfavouring
Locked in modefications
trying to water down the
aLL mEN whilst desperately
championing the Equality of
Constitution sentimentally
seperated mU made American
wORDing of the separating
advocated the same in the
inFANTiLe Constitution
separating, seperated
locked early into hiS
to (M)Other nATURE
wife and 4 out of 5
{FH} having lost a
no different from
too a Sentimentalist
Jefferson {TJ} he

$$\{i\}=\Sigma[(1^70)+\{1^{71}2\}]^n=\{\text{☰}\}$$

d-aCT II's

d-aCT I's

$$\{i\}=\Sigma[(1^{7}0)^{*}\{1^{7}0\}^{*}(1^{7}0)]^{n}=(\text{⊞})$$

(Hume}) didn't quite get iT
right too. He got iT the wrong
way round, poor old (Hume}) Little
did he twig that we each a face-less
impression are in fact a two bodied
idea of the constant conjunction of
an ever present faceful (m)Other
and (f)Other pair that makes our
Adult passions purely then
the slave of our inFANTILE
Reasons Poor (David})
he was truely mixed
and did indeed not
get iT the right
way round

One and All
universally fit for
in the making of a World
of it's Adult Passions and
as regards ridding infantile Reason
Imperative to be totaly inadequate
and {f}Other pair revealing his Categorical
uniTY of one of an ever present faceful (m)Other
simply a copied impression of the full bodied
twig that his Transcendental uniTY is
beYONDs Poor old {Kant)} little did he
d-eMPTiNESS of our bACKs and
in iT's Self purely partakes of the
Transcendental uniFYing Thing in
his Categorically weigh'd down
certainly all his But as regards
mANiFoLD of perceptions was
to iT! Aperception Yes! His
There ain't no uniTY
correction of (Hume})
get iT right too in his
{Kant)} didn't quite

$$\{i\}=\Sigma[\{1{}^{5}04'\}{}^{*}(1{}^{71}2){}^{*}\{1{}^{5}04'\}]^{n}=\{\equiv\}$$

d-aCT II's

d-aCT I's

$$\{i\}=\Sigma[(1^70)+\{1^{31}3\}]^n=\{\equiv\}$$

{Aristotle} as was said
earlier didn't quite get iT
He too got iT the wrong way
round poor old {Aristotle} Little did
he twig that in "saying of" Plato's fORMs
that they necessarily had to be "present
in" some primary concrete substance
like a man or a horse before
they could ever bE unlike
the constantly conjoined free
floating fORMs present in
the fullsome in-between
of the d-eMPTY bACK
& beYOND Poor {Aristotle}
he was truely mixed and
did indeed not get iT
round the right wAY

to bE
oRDER
and mE in
hAVE yOU
still have had to
would necessarily
bACK and beYOND
out the d-eMPTiNESS of his
oNE or LoCKean mANY cluttering
diNG an siCH whether a bERKLYAN
Little did he twig that his puTATiVE
{Aristotle}'s rag bag of cATEGORiES
the number of coNCEPTs "present in"
right too in his tinkering with the
{Kant)} didn't quite get iT

$$\{i\}=\Sigma[\{1^504'\}*(1^{71}2)*\{1^504'\}]^n=\{\Xi\}$$

d-aCT I's

d-aCT I's

$$\{i\}=\Sigma[(1^{31}3).\{1^{4}04'\}]^{n}=\{\text{☵}\}$$

{Fichte} and {Schelling}
both intellectual busy
body son's of {Kant)}
both mANiFoLD
products of raw
inTUITioNs and
grounded both in
their own inFANTiLe
tan-trumatic wAYs
ended going their
own separate wAYs
{Fichte} having located
& pOSITioned him-sELF
absolutely central to
his mANiFoLD of aCTs
of reJECTion hE the
LorD and mASTER of his
own separate mANiFoLD
bundled and cATEGORiSeD
solely by him there being no
oTHER but him the iCH bin
mein iCH a {f}Other Landed
Deutsche iCH bin iCH

oTHERing iCH
iCH bin mein und sein
absolutely groundless
creation of that uncondition'd
by him-sELF the totally condition'd
iNTUITIONs bundled & cATEGORiSeD
his own separate mANiFoLD of raw
the productive Lord and mASTER of
acceptance he the sERVANT of
of acts of reJECTIOn and
identificatory mANiFoLD
absolutely central to his
and pOSITioned the oTHER
contrary to {Fichte} located
separate ways {Schelling}
ended going their own
own inFANTiLe wAYs
grounded both in their
of raw inTUITioNs and
mANiFoLD products
body son's of {Kant)} both
both intellectual busy
{Schelling} and (Fichte}

$\{i\}=\Sigma[(1^7 0).\{1^7 04'\}]^n=\{\equiv\}$

d-aCT II's

d-aCT II's

$$[U]=[1^404']=[\text{☷}]$$

**And Look @
this toothless Lot
this Academic and
emasculated 4th Estate Lot
who will write and publish
anything that guarantees
them both job security
and a Big Fat Pension**

Pension Funds
hedge funded Personal
projected values of their
purely for the sake of the
[m]e-O-LiberaL Capitalism
following the LoGic of
out Political Servants
to the Teeth and droned
Political Servants armed
Lot their Right and Left
self-seving ways of this
And take a Look @ the

$$[U]=[1^7 04']=[\equiv]$$

d-aCT I's

d-aCT I's

$$\{i\}=\Sigma[\{1^70\}^*(1^704')]^n=(\equiv)$$

ShiVa loves fcuKing
hiS beloved Shakti
oTHERLY pARVATi
whilst sHE hiS
Shaktii
loVingly
does the
birthing
of wORLDS
(m)aNskrit'd
wORLDS
within
wORLDs
and cOUNT
LeSS Otherlies
not yet to
CoME

his wORDs
the coming of
oNEs prior to
oNANismic
mirroring the
oTHERLies
iMAGEGiNARY
oTHER wORLDed
fuLLY in unspoken
cLiMaXing eVENT
wORLDs joYously
wORLDs within
inFORMed mU
words of oTHERLY
his (m)aNskrit'd
sUBstance to his
endlessly giVing
ShiVa whilst
oTHERLY fcuKer
fcuKing hER
pARVATi loves

$$\{i\}=\Sigma[\{1^70\}*(1^70)]^n=(\boxplus)$$

d-aCT II's

d-aCT II's

$$\{i\}=\Sigma[(1^70).\{1^704'\}]^n=\{\equiv\}$$

{sOREN}'s
major [m]ULess
point no different
from {K)}'s was that
eXisTence was not
a prediCATE so
after faithlessly
dumping {rEGiNA}
hE LePT from
hiS seLF pre
diCATING
pivotal point
of eXisTence
into the arms
of his aLL
approving
substitute
{F}OTHER
he could
do no
other

exiSTense
of (_)UmaN
ness of the whole
of the pOINTLess
pointLess point
pushed forward the
Less adULTescence
the whole of his (m)u
(sARTRE) throughout
inFANTiLe eXisTence
of hiS aNGST ridden
pivotal thought
ness bEiNG the
nOTHING

$$\{i\}=\Sigma[\{1^70\}+(1^71)]^n=(\equiv)$$

d-aCT II's

d-aCT I's

$$\{i\}=\Sigma[\{1^70\}+(1^{71}2)]^n=(\text{三})$$

(cEORAN) a fellow
Parisean Existant
having bracked himself
off from a domineering
d-littling and demeaning
pair in Infancy inevitably
found The Trouble with
Being Born forever
troubling his polished
(mad)Adultescent
Texts prove

ShiVa
& demeaning
domineeering
Shakti he her
demeaning
d-littling and
cases she his
indeed in both
(cEORAN)'s case
troubling in
have been
would
Worker
Tantrick Sex
part-time Hindu
& demeaned DaLiT
d-littled domineeered
the likes of {Indhira} a
happy encounter with
holidaying mutually
Even some

$$(i)=\Sigma[(1^{7}0)+\{1^{71}2\}]^{n}=\{\equiv\}$$

d-aCT II's

d-aCT I's

$$[U]=[1^{71}2)]=[\text{☰}]$$

**Look @ the innocent
greened out Lot happily
awaiting the arrival of
their Promised Land**

Pension Funds
hedge funded Personal
projected values of their
purely for the sake of the
[m]e-O-LiberaL cAPiTALiSM
following the LoGic of
out Political Servants
to the Teeth and droned
Political Servants armed
Lot their Right and Left
self-serving ways of this
And take a Look @ the

$$[U]=[1^7 04']=[\equiv]$$

d-aCT II's

d-aCT I's

$$\{i\}=\Sigma[\{1^70\}+(1^{31}3)]^n=(\equiv)$$

(Hume})'s
auld Reekie
frien' (Adam)
a have-not
advocated it
necessary in
Adulthood to
constantly
truck trade
and barter in
a' bloody
thing
both
within
& without
that interest
full rentfull
LaBOURing
eCONOMY
of survival
owned by
aLL that
[h]Add

that [h]aVe
owned by aLL
of [m]Exploitation
LaBOURing eCONOMY of
and resulted in a debt fuLL
have-noTs spending power
to a drop in the value of aLL
fiAT that has led increasingly
supply simply by clickable
their Master's owned Money
the increasing of their's and
increasingly advocating
sales mark ups whilst
attached to indecent
and barter in GooDs
Others to truck trade
their view for aLL
necessary in
economically
[h]Add found it
both oNEs that
buddy (Friedman}
{Leo}'s Chicago

$$\{i\}=\Sigma[\{(1^{31}3)^*\{1^404'\}]^n=\{\equiv\}$$

d-aCT I's

d-aCT I's

$$[U]=[1^704']=[\equiv]$$

**The wEST won beating
those eASTERN cOLD War
COMMUNIST [m]Other fCUKERs
diALECTiCAL [m]Other fCUKERs who
wiped their own arse with both hANDs
LosT and LoRDED over now though
by the domineering Right handed
LoGiC of CaPiTAL**

taking oVER
increasingly
with Machines
utility now though
Das Capital of marginal
so well in his master tEXT
that he explored and critiqued
of MaRX's Labour Theory of Value
sons of AdAM SmiTH the {f}Other
[m)Other fCUKERs. All ageing
Cold wESTERN CaPITALIST
The eAST Lost lost to those

$$[U]=[1^7 04']=[\equiv]$$

d-aCT II's

d-aCT I's

$$\{i\}=\Sigma[\{1^{7}04'\}*(1^{7}0)*\{1^{7}04'\}]^{n}=\{\equiv\}$$

{Hegel)}'s criticism of {Spinoza}
double aspected (Spinoza) was
that he had not bothered to
tarry with the negative. It
was really his way of saying
that (Spinoza} missed out
in a way of sequencing the
arrival of his putative modes
of {Diva} ve (Natura)
re-christened the
{World Spirit}
by {Hegel)}
The way
according
to {Hegel)}
was diALECTiCAL
in nature grounded in
the Oedipal-like marriage
of two place (m)Otherly Thesis's
with one place {f}Otherly anti
Thesis's & the births of umpteen
three place Contradictions {Aristotle}
would have been horrified

LOGiC
& incomplete
LoVE's inconsistent
explain inFANTiLE
dG has attempted to
the [Look@_] request

hAViNG and throwing in
two place [_have_] one of
predicate of bEiNG & the
adding in the two place [_am_]
his three LoGiCAL signs and by
By mirroring (Frege})'s use of

LoGiCAL reduction of nUMBERs
& the 2nd natural set [oNE] in his
namely the empty 1st null set
gRAB-bAG sets of cANTOR's
the first two fundamental
implication he then added in
that of the if[if]then one of
sign of negation along with
sign of identity and the til[-]de
field of LoGiC to the equ[=]als
After (Frege}) had reduced the

$\{i\}=\Sigma[(1^4 04')^*\{1^{31}3\}^*(1^4 04')]^n=(\text{≡})$

d-aCT II's

d-aCT I's

$$\{i\}=\Sigma[\{1^70\}^*(1^704')^n=(\equiv)$$

Charles {Saunders)
a tan-trumatically
driven New World mAN
couldn't stop thinking
peircing thinkings of
thought oUT thinkings
throughout his (m)A
{d})adULTescence
hAViNG triadically
tuppled his inFANTile
mANIFOLD into the
LooK at (m)E
I have iT

& I am iT
mEsome
moded
3-some

LoVe
& (m)UNIVERSAL
bundled thoughts
Logic of triadically
in the bundling
grounding iT aLL
in later Life by
chanced his Luck
iT threesome he
I have iT and I am
into the LooK at (m)E
inFANTile mANIFOLD
having "congealed" hiS
out his (m)ADULTescence
oUT thinkings through
thinkings of thought
thinking peircing
of mine couldn't stop
'congealed' thought
driven New World
a tan-trumatically
Charles {Saunders)

$$\{i\}=\Sigma[\{1\,^7 0\}^*(1\,^7 04')]^n=(\equiv)$$

d-aCT II's

d-aCT I's

$$\{i\}=\Sigma[(1^70)+\{1^{31}3\}]^n=\{\equiv\}$$
{Aristotle} in
his thought out
thinkings *'noesis*
noeseos noesis'
thought that
he got iT with his
4 syllogistic Forms hiS
All Some Every and *None*
along with his *excluded middle*
not not not and not not. No! he did
not. [oNE] place predicate {Aristotle}
did not get iT [tWo] place predicate
(Frege}) could have told him that
but then again (Frege}) was no
different. He was far from being
consistent and complete
{Russell)} set him right
on that point

side their thinking biTs
endlessly do the same in
fellow confused creatures
other than our own in which
creating and caring for Worlds
He simply avoids iT by endlessly
before the existence of Time
was confused by that one long
even God the {Father}
Confused? No worries
contains iT's own Self
not contain themselves
all those sets that do
the set that contains
simply asking whether
(Frege}) right by
{Russell)} had set

$$\{i\}=\Sigma[\{1^404'\}^*(1^{31}3)^*\{1^404'\}]^n=\{\Xi\}$$

d-aCT II's

d-aCT I's

$$\{i\}=\Sigma[(1^31)+\{1^{31}3\}]^n=\{\equiv\}$$

**{Ludwig}'s conclusion
was that hE was simply
aLL show**

just such a showing!
simply hiS rejection of
{Alan}'s last biT(e) was

$$\{i\}=\Sigma[(1^7 0).\{1^7 04'\}]^n=\{\equiv\}$$

d-aCT II Sc II's

d-aCT II Sc II's

$$(i)=\Sigma[(1^70)^*\{1^704'\}]^n=\{\equiv\}$$

(She} belted her neck
to the bedpost his belt
and simply stepped off
and dangled two centimetres
from the ground. A seeming act
of abandonment. Her two year
old Elif her (br)Other's
her (m)Other indeed
the whole World
iT was not! she was
simply abandoning
the rejecting oTHER
within. iT had long
gone too far

gone too far
iT had long
oNE Sadly
rejecting
& every non
rejecting each
she was forever
rejecting oNE within
abandoned her own
never having ever
{m}Other understood
disapproved
criTiCALLY
unfavored
inFANTiLY
{Nurset} her

$$(i)=\Sigma[(1^7 0/4').\{1^7 0/4'\}]^n=\{\ddots\}$$

d-aCT II's

d-aCT I's

$$(i)=\Sigma[\{1\,^7 0\}^*(1\,^7 1)^*\{1\,^7 0\}]^n=\{\text{⊞}\}$$

{Halldis)} who appeared to
have everything. Physical beauty
She'd been the University Beauty
Queen of her University Year
Social standing. She a Doctor
A big Muckle Farmer husband
A beautiful bunch of kids and
yet here she's answering

'Don't Look @ (m)E
I don't have iT
and I'm not iT'

How could that ever bE
Simple what U say U are has
nothing to do with U're present
day circumstances iT's a trace
of U're inFANTILE past

That was the first major
break through and boy
was iT pleasing

unlike her Mum's
(Him) Turkey her fate
Dad's mattered little to
he made his judgement
conscience free viewing
playing with both. After a
video footage of her 'happily'
a fortnight in order to establish
Judge postponed his judgement for
the Authorities knew her views the
lock me up and leave (m)E alone'
'Put Nurset and Seckin in the Bin
his work was done. She cared
to Turkey. What did he care
the Buggers can send her back
barely 2 then. Yes! he thought
her own Mum's Suicide. She was
the Local Authorities following
the one assigned to her by
her Mummy carer substitute
her Dad returned her to Annie
(She} said to Annie her carer as
and Daddy loves (m)E'
'You love Daddy

$$\{i\}=\Sigma[\{1^{7}0\}^{*}(1^{7}04')]^{n}=(\equiv)$$

d-aCT I's

d-aCT I's

$$\{i\}=\Sigma[(1^70)+\{1^71\}]^n=\{\boxplus\}$$

**Murderous {Dirac} a
modern day materialist
in his exploration of
Mathematical Space
nowhere better to go
found a place for
an anti-Particle
within Physical
Space....fancy
that!**

Space
Perceptual
hole of hiS
domineered
like the facial
fall fourth not un
fORMs domineeringly
pLATONiC number
which his favoured
Space through
Mathematical
found a hole in
his exploration
(GödeL) in

$$\{i\}=\Sigma[\{1^{7}0\}+(1^{7}1)]^{n}=(\overline{\overline{}})$$

d-aCT II's

d-aCT I's

$$\{i\}=\Sigma[\{1^{6}04'\}*(1^{7}1)*\{1^{6}04'\}]^{n}=\{\equiv\}$$

Following his Formal
castration by (GödeL)
through the use of
his Incompleteness
Theory and his discovery
then that numbers weren't
simple 'Empty Forms' but had
substance. Substance that must
not and will not do as Formal
Mathematicians like himself
expected. Nasty little buggers
who certainly knew their place
{Hilbert)} went on to then
have his Intuitionist rival
{Brouwer) a long believer in
the unformalizable nature of
mathematical thought kicked
off the editorial board of the
Mathematische Annale
Journal Nasty big
bugger who didn't
know his place

him though!
he didn't cross
around Bet dG's glad
there's few like them
the pair hadn't met
{br}Other of mine. Pity
brilliant past-present
eVENTs {Brouwer) a
World of present and past
a Mathematical gRAB-bAG
as dG has done and create
middle from his World just
exclude (Aristotle)'s excluded
feared to tread. He wanted to
and go where others like {Hilbert)}
but he wanted to take things further
he was free to have such a thought
like hiS fellow Topologist {br}Others
thrown out Euclid's 5th Postulate just
as to the actual shape of Space having
unlike {Hilbert)} he was intrigued
the worst out in {Hilbert)}
words. He certainly brought
the worst out in people. His
{Brouwer) brought

$\{i\}=\Sigma[\{1^{71}2\}^*(1^504')]^n=\{\Xi\}$

d-aCT II's

d-aCT II Sc I's

$$\{i\}=\Sigma[(1^{31}3).\{1^{4}04'\}]^{n}=\{\equiv\}$$

{Socrates} unlike
{Wittgenstein}
did not get iT
His way of
philosophy
was his own
b-littling
critical
excuse for
dialectically
Questioning
all oTHERs

{dA}SEiNweLT End
to an an old new
things through
unable to think
did not get iT too
weLT (Heidegger)
Land (mA)SEiN
mein Deutsche
(Heidegger)
(mA)SEiNweLT
iCH bin mein
(Heidegger)

$$\{i\}=\Sigma[\{1^3 1\}.(1^6 04')]^n=(\equiv)$$

d-aCT I's

d-aCT I's

$$\{i\}=\Sigma[(1^31).\{1^604'\}]^n=\{\equiv\}$$

**Immersed
in zERO-Less
Greek numbers
2nd Century
{Plotinus}
insisted that
the oNE...the
foundational oNE
transcended both
sPACE and tiME no
different from 17th
Century {Kant)} and
his unbound by
sPACE and tiME
transcendental
[m]Unifying
"diNG an siCH"**

{f}Other
wiLLfull
of her own
representation
mUfully chosen
own (m)Other's
{f}Other his
by his contrarian
& Schopenhauered
his contrarian (m)Other
in his inFANTescence by
oNE was {Arthur}'d
and rePRESENTATiON
"diNG an siCH" as wiLL
the post-Kantian
Schopenhauer

$\{i\}=\Sigma[(1^7 1).\{1^6 04'\}]^n=\{\equiv\}$

d-aCT I's

d-aCT I's

$$\{i\}=\Sigma[\{1^71\}+\{1^70\}+\{1^{31}2\}$$
$$\{1^31\}+\{1^{71}2\}+(1^70)]^n=(\boxplus)$$

a tEONTRiCKAL saying

".....tHAT hooks it aLL up
the wiLL of gOD...you call it
Jesus...call it Mohammed...call it
Gooby BoB...call it Nuclear Mind
call it blow the World up...call
it your Heart...whatever
you call it it's still
Music to {m}E
it's there it's
the wiLL of LiFE"

from the mouth of
Man's's Son will
fully denied
a pAYBack
dEATH

rAZOR"
dEATH
a pAYBack

close to {m}E
& if you get to
a jUG of wiNE
hoBO a bOXCAR
tRAMP a bUM a
noBODY a
"I's a
hiS
oNE of
knowing
unknowing
anoTHER

$$\{1^31\}+\{1^{71}2\}+(1^70)]^n=(\boxplus)$$
$$\{i\}=\Sigma[\{1^71\}+\{1^70\}+\{1^{31}2\}$$

d-aCT II's

d-aCT III's

$$\{i\}=\Sigma[\{1^{31}3\}+(1^{31}3)]^n=(\equiv)$$

(Parmenides)
Eleatic God-like
(m)Other had hiM

hE could never
have had hER

just as hE
could never
not bE iT
for her as
she for him
both were
oNE for each
oTHER

the thought
of not bEiNG
such a oNE
impossible
for each

hood
Lot in child
(Heraclitus)'s

same twice
never the
going daily
coming and
bECOMiNGs
hAViNGs and
streams of

& d-littlement
oNE of domination
ridden Ephesus
His a strife

$$\{i\}=\Sigma[\{1^{7}1\}+(1^{3}1)]^{n}=(\equiv)$$

d-aCT III's

d-aCT I's

$$\{i\}=\Sigma[\{1^71\}+(1^70)]^n=(\vcenter{\hbox{$\substack{\blacksquare\blacksquare\\\blacksquare\blacksquare}$}})$$

an aNCiENT
Greek's son's
ontological
saying
" the first principles
of the uNiVERSE are
aTOMs and eMPTY
sPACE everything
else is merely
oPiNiON"

oPiNiON
else merely"
"everything
fEYNMAN's

yet to bE"
pARTiCLEs
of wAViNG
of sPACE fiELDs
each fills the whole
but qUANTUM fiELDs
"there is nothing

mODERN one
another more

$$\{i\}=\Sigma[\{1^70\}.(1^704')]^n=(\equiv)$$

d-aCT I's

d-aCT I's

$$\{i\}=\Sigma[\{1^{71}2\}^{*}(1^{5}04')]^{n}=\{\Xi\}$$

Think @ how {Brouwer) the
domineered and demeaned number
invigorated One of a domineering
and demeaning elder {br}Other
preferring {f}Others must have felt
when first appointed to the editorial
board of one of the most respected
journals within the Mathematical
World namely the 'Mathematische
Annale' Journal and how his
feelings had later turned when
kicked off the said editorial board
upon the recommendation
of a far more favoured
Board meMBER

inTUITIONs
bending Mathematical
mIND and tOPOLOGICAL
egged him on to greater
and worst in him and
brought out the best
Board Members had
decision of his fellow
such an unfavouring
And think @ how

$$[U]=[1^5 04']=[\Xi]$$

d-aCT I's

d-aCT II's

$$\{i\}=\Sigma[(1^70)^*\{1^71\}]^n=\{\boxminus\}$$

(Hitler}
iCH bin
Deutsche
Land uber Als
(Hitler} got
iT unlike
(Heidegger)
hE thought
things through
to an old new {dA}
SEiNweLT End

take iT
just had to
player who
second Act
homoerotic
submissive
figure hE the
(Hitler} type
domineering
d-aCT II
dressed up
from some
probably
though
the virus
he did get
old new end
through to an
things suspiciously
despite thinking
did not get iT
{Foucault}

$\{i\}=\Sigma[(1^7 1).\{1^6 04'\}]^n=\{\equiv\}$

d-aCT II's

d-aCT II's

$$\{i\}=\Sigma[\{1^{7}0/4'\}+(1^{7}0/4')]^{n}=(\text{☱})$$

(Nietszche)
the archetypal
{d}AFiA & (m)AFiA'd
inFANTiLE oNE
rejected by his
adULTescent
(Salome)
grasped
fully the
nature
of critically
disapproving
(m)Uber
wENSCH
pOWER

rePRESENTATiONs
(m)Otherly wORLD
like ways of his
mANiCHEAN
the wiLL-fuLL
too obsessed with
didn't quite get iT far
{Schopenhouer}

$$\{i\}=\Sigma[(1^71).\{1^604'\}]^n=\{\equiv\}$$

d-aCT I's

d-aCT II's

$$\{i\}=\Sigma[(1^71)^*\{1^70\}^*(1^71)]^n=(\boxplus)$$

(Saul}) was (Saul}) happy
with his (m)Other's chosen
name Saul He would have no
truck with that other Saul
Saul Kripke and his 'rigid
designators' and other Worlds
This piss awful World was
all that there is. Consistently
Schopenhourian his views
and once was enough
Thank you!

{br}Others
more favoured
all *rigidly designated*
the further torment of
Worlds all necessary in
and other Worlds Other
regards 'rigid designators'
had laid down the Law as
that other (Saul} who
(Saul} Kripke was

$$\{i\}=\Sigma[(1^{71}2)^*\{1^504'\}]^n=\{\equiv\}$$

d-aCT II's

d-aCT II's

$$\{i\}=\Sigma\,[(1^71)^*\{1^70\}^*(1^71)]^n=(\boxplus)$$

Think @ how (Saul})
that domineered (m)Other
rigid superiored One must
have felt after meeting with
the famed archDuke Atheist
{Richard Dwakin}'s at the last
Group meeting of his College's
Debating Society {Richard} that
arch rigid gene reductionist who
happily agreed with (Saul})
that night that 'once was far
more than enough'
Thank you!

Thank yoU!
Appearance necessary
One Judgement only One
One God One Death
'once was enough' belief
had all agreed with him in his
his beloved Debating Group
the Believer section of
And think @ how

$$[U]=[1^504']=[\equiv]$$

d-aCT I's

d-aCT II's

$$\{i\}=\Sigma[(1^71)^*\{1^604'\}]^n=\{\equiv\}$$

**BoobFuLL yet
pestered now
with the standing
presence of his diCK
poor Miss Bertie stuck
in d-aCT II totally
oblivious of d-aCTs
III and IV yet
to come**

to come
III and IV yet
oblivious of d-aCTs
stuck in d-aCT II totally
poor Master Mabel
her Lack of a diCK
pestered now with
BoobLess yet

$$(i)=\Sigma[\{1^71\}+(1^71)]^n=(\boxminus)$$

d-aCT II's

d-aCT I's

$$\{i\}=\Sigma[(1^70)+\{1^71\}]^n=\{\boxminus\}$$

{dA} {dA} {dA}
dUm the coming
of frightfuL
{dA} fuLL
sounds

sounds
of {dA} dUmb
the mASTER
{Beethoven}

$$\{i\}=\Sigma[(1^70)+\{1^71\}]^n=\{\text{▦}\}$$

d-aCT II's

d-aCT I's

$$\{i\}=\Sigma[(1^70)^*\{1^70\}^*(1^70)]^n=(\boxplus)$$

(Monet}) preferred his oUTsides
to his inSIDES...after squeezing out
aLL thought...he simply de-picted
iT aLL then in paint Lovingly
placing each biT of colour
next to iT's mate. If the
matching did not suit
smudged oUT
and canvas
tossed aside

process
eAR in the
unSEEiNG
cutting off an
aLL in paint
fULLness of iT
against the utter
{van Gough)} rAGEd

$$\{i\}=\Sigma[\{1^7 1\}*(1^7 0)*\{1^7 1\}]^n=\{\text{☲}\}$$

d-aCT II's

d-aCT I's

$$\{i\}=\Sigma[(1^704')^*\{1^70\}^*(1^704')]^n=(\equiv)$$

(Wagner}) similarly
preferred his oUTsides to
his inSIDES...after silencing aLL
thought...he simply noted iT aLL
then in dressed - up sounds
placing each biT of sound
next to iT's mate If the
matching did not suit
music scored out
and costumes
tossed aside

process
ears in the
aLL rAGEFUL
shutting off
bITs of sounds
aLL in mINIMAL
fULLness of iT
in the utter
cAGED
(REICH)

$$\{i\}=\Sigma[\{1^71\}.(1^604')]^n=(\equiv)$$

d-aCT I's

d-aCT II's

$$\{i\}=\Sigma[(1^{31}3)+\{1^{31}3\}]^{n}=\{\equiv\}$$

**bLOCKed from
having by both he
{tULLY} bLOCKed out
such abstract thoughts
in dullish bLOCKs
of paint**

absent Queens
kiNGs and
aBSOLUTiST
d-LiTTLiNG
b-LiTTLiNG
or otherwise
that of like-minded
Governance rather than
the people" in their own
the "sovereign will of
cRiTiCOCRATiC ways of
knowingly the d-aCT II
aDULTescence un
he championed in
loving {f}OTHER
ways of his single
knowing b-littling
birth and the un
(m)OTHER in child
the death of his
from having by
blocked both
hE {Rousseau}

$\{i\}=[\{1^{31}3\}]^{n}=\{\equiv\}$

d-aCT II's

d-aCT II's

$$\{i\}=\Sigma[(1^70)^*\{1^31\}^*(1^70)]^n=(\text{⁞⁞})$$

Think @ how le bon
David decieved infantilely
in Love (Hume}) no different
from le bon {Descartes)} must
have felt upon discovering on his
invited 1763 Paris Trip as the
celebrated 'Scottish Enlightenment'
new gROUPie that he needed
other Men before he could come
Threesome's were his thing He first
needed a her a Madame de Boufflers
her in his case to love a him a {Rousseau}
him that would in turn love such a loving
Madame de Boufflers her so that he
David could in turn love her Madame de
Boufflers too just like his {Rousseau}
him. Boy must he have come then
it's all in the bracket's
no le bon head just
take a Look

(Hume})
affair with
botched English
Boufflers-less
Madame de
cRATiC
cRiTiCO
following his
return to France
have felt upon his
{Rousseau} must
also @ how
And think

$$\{i\}=\Sigma[\{1^{31}3\}]^n=\{\equiv\}$$

d-aCT II's

d-aCT I's

$$\{i\}=\Sigma[(1^{7}0)*\{1^{71}2\})]^{n}=\{\equiv\}$$

An addend
Um to his list
(She} a drunk
Amie Winehouse
makeover who
prefered Europeans
He fingered her
lovingly rather
than enter a study
in wUmanhood
probably
his best

married with 2 kids
& found her Mum's true love
she explored Australia House's
totally rejected by her Dad
beans of her Uncle's abuse
Following the spilling of the

and her Mum's little secret
emigrated to Australia (Doreen}
She didn't him. Her true love had
Her Dad had absolutely adored her
Mum had died when she was 5
we all are by then (Doreen} 's
connecting up. Programmed
bits of hardware have stopped
the age of 5 our little dendritic

& I am iT But Why? Simple by

resolute Look@(m)E I have it
same period (Doreen} was a
abused by her throughout the
{br}Other and domineered and
from 5 until 14 by her stepmum's
regularly abused sexually
Despite having been

$$(i)=\Sigma[\{1^7 0\}^*(1^7 04')]^n=(\equiv)$$
d-aCT II's

d-aCT II's

$$[U]=[1^{31}2]=[\equiv]$$

**They tried to
kiLL uS they failed
Let's eAT**

**Think @ how
mascaraded
{Arabella) must
have felt when first
eATing with (Ariella}'s
West Banked Grandfather
knowing full well that iT
could have been her own
Grandfather that had gassed
his {br}Others and when
shown the perimeters
of the Grandfather's
new fencing and that
of his neighbouring
Group of fellow
Settlers**

beyond
fully lived
that riGHT
of their owners
dogs and the eYE
avoid the Palestinian
and a lot more able to
their domineering fencing
had felt much safer behind
of (Ariella}'s Grandfather
and fenced in neighbours
the newly fenced off
And think @ how

Let's fCUK
They'll fail

to kiLL uS
are trying
They

$[U]=[1^31]=[\equiv]$

d-aCT I's

d-aCT I's

$$(i)=\Sigma[\{1\,^{6}04'\}^{*}(1\,^{7}1)^{*}\{1\,^{6}04'\}]^{n}=\{\equiv\}$$

Think @ how {Phyllis)} the
stripper after a decent night's
work must feel when placarded
yet again by a group of
Evangelical Christians
reminding her that her
eND is NiGH and that she
needs to mend the error
of her ways before
catching her Last
Bus Home

their [m]ULess ways
and confronting the errors of
www.piecingitalltogether.co.uk
feel after Googling and visiting
of Evangelical Christians will
And think @ how this group

$[U]=[1^504']=[\Xi]$

d-aCT II's

d-aCT I's

$$\{i\}=\Sigma[(1^70)+\{1^{31}3\}]^n=\{\equiv\}$$

Look @ how {Jahandar}
a Western Trained {f}Otherly
b-littled Particle Physicist must
have felt when first accepted
into the Iranian Uranium 235
enrichment programme and
for what purpose? That
was no concern of his!
b-littling muLLAH
{f}Other substitutes
were far better
equipped to decide
on maTTERs
such as That

Energy Agency Group
the International Atomic
of any visitor from the IAEA
of the questions and directives
unequipped to satisfy any
{Jahandar} was equally
And think @ how

$$[U]=[1^504']=[\text{☲}]$$

d-aCT I's

d-aCT I's

$$\{i\}=\Sigma[(1^{7}0)^{*}\{1^{7}04'\}]^{n}=\{\equiv\}$$

Lacking
what pleased
(Lacan} looked
for iT in the
Speech of the
oTHER
after having
inverted
de Saussure's
Signified
Signifier
pair Dream's
condensates &
displacements
signified little
for (h}iM unlike
{h}iS mASTER
Chains of Signifiers
a l'Abhinavagupta
suggestive
Signifiers
was where
iT was aT

(h}E made little
sense of them
though despite
(h}iS knowledge of
the Infantile mIRROR
Phase silly Little
bIG mAN (h}E
ought to have
just asked in the
silence of (h}iS
sittings "What
sort of I are yoU
I am iT or I'm not
iT I have iT or I
don't have iT?"
{Popper} would
have Looked
aT (h}iM then
making sense
of iT aLL that's
for sure!

$$\{i\}=\Sigma[(1^70)^*\{1^704'\}]^n=\{\equiv\}$$

d-aCT I's

d-aCT I's

$$\{i\}=\Sigma[\{1^704'\}*(1^70)*\{1^704'\}]^n=\{\equiv\}$$

**Having been
terrorized by the
sAVAGE ways of his
d-aCT II miNORs
mULess {Burke)}
championed a mU
lessly unworkable
cONSERVATiVE
re-run of the
d-aRiSTOCRATiC
ways of his
fellow d-aCT
I mAJORs**

and sUBLiME
the bEAUTiFUL
the nature of
the cultivation of
miNORs thro'
mAJORs and
of d-aCTs I & II
of the sensuous ways
aESTHETiC re-education
the mUlessly unworkable
terror championed
post d-aCT II
in his mUless
{Schiller}

$$\{i\}=\Sigma[(1^70).\{1^704'\}]^n=\{\equiv\}$$

d-aCT I's

d-aCT II Sc I's

$$\{i\}=\Sigma[(1^7 0)^*\{1^7 04'\}]^n=\{\equiv\}$$

**Think @ how (Galileo}
must have felt walking away
from his Inquisitorial Accusers
after recanting his theory that
the Earth moved around the Sun
muttering the Words**
'E pur si muove'

yet moved
yet that the tHiNG
Life not having sussed
Grace to House Arrest for
sentence by their God's
felt commuting his Prison
of Accusers must have
his Inquisitorial Group
And think @ how

$$[U]=[1^704']=[\equiv]$$

d-aCT I's

d-aCT II Sc II's

$$\{i\}=\Sigma[\{1^70\}*(1^70)*\{1^70\}]^n=\{\boxminus\}$$

{Hugh)} was trashed by
by both and by {h}is
scientifically bemused
QuantumMechanical
{br}Others 'mULTi
vERSE get rEAL oNE's
enough' Fags Food
& Drink his way
forward then
leading to
a 52 year
old death

Burned
& then
trashed
by the Bin
Men {his)}
last defiant
wish in this
oNE at least!

at least!
in this oNE
pleasing wish
last {d}ADDY
Men (Her}
by the Bin
her own life
after taking
like {h}iM
trashed just
burned and
entirely {h}iS
Everett was
LittLe Lizzie
his daughter
(Elizabeth}

$$(i)=\Sigma[(1^70)^*\{1^704'\}]^n=\{\equiv\}$$

d-aCT II Sc II's

d-aCT I's

$$(i)=\Sigma[(1^70)+\{1^{31}3\}]^n=\{\equiv\}$$

Think @ how wee baby
Abike's b-littled and for ever
colonised Nigerian {Mum} had felt
after learning that Abike her newly
vaccinated daughter had been his last
before having his doctor head chopped
off by oNE of her mIND colonising Islamic
Boko Harem {br}Others & sisters
that 'Western Education
is Sacrilege' Boko
Harem Lot

covered Lot
domineering Godly
their Work amongst such a
possibly thought of continueing
Medical colleagues could have
of remaining North Korean
And think @ how his Group

$$[U]=[1^704']=[\equiv]$$

d-aCT I's

d-aCT I's

$$(i)=\Sigma[(1^7 0)^*\{1^{71}2\}]^n=\{\equiv\}$$

**Take a Look
@ how (Amie}
the shriveled up past
Lover of John her first
Group Leader must
have felt when John
had passsed her over
for some sleek young
recruiT tHiNG**

young tHiNGs
tend to go for sleek
all Group Leaders
And Look @ how

$$[U]=[1^604']=[\equiv]$$

d-aCT I's

$$\{i\}=\Sigma[(1^70)+\{1^70\}]^n=\{⠿\}$$

Lacking
what pleased
the philosophically
inclined LooK for
iT in aLL of iT
{ZiZEK} is oNE
an intolerantly
displeasing oNE
a biT like his
master {HeGeL)}
silly little bIG man
hE ought to just sit
sit in the midst of
the empty bACK
and beYOND of
his suBLimely
suggestive
(m)Udeological
Texts Lackanian
off-shoots & LooK
for iT then in
LoVe's LoGiC

wORLDS of wAR
end for eVERmore
Arlene's in order to
LoGiC hiS own and
makings of LoVe's
and worked out the
being Triniity tested
have just sat after
man hE ought to
silly little bIG
World War II
his worrisome
tHiNG to end
a bIG nUmbered
in the makings of
Almos oNE lost

pleasing Los
an intolerantly
{Feynman} was oNE
for iT in biTs of iT
inclined LooK
the scientifically
what pleased
Lacking

$\{i\}=\Sigma[(1^70)+\{1^70\}]^n=\{\vdots\vdots\}$

d-aCT I's

d-aCT II's

$$\{i\}=\Sigma[(1^70)+\{1^71\}]^n=\{\equiv\}$$

{Selahattin}
a Kurdish frame
Less canvas of
fleeting impressions
uncanvased by {hIM} a
series of thought-prints
before {hE} shot
and killed

[cr]iSiSfuLLY
slaughtered
as THEY shot and
of fleeting impressions
canvasless facefuLLs
thought-prints
Less series of
They a fACE

$[U]=[1^6 04']=[\equiv]$

d-aCT I's

d-aCT I's

$$\{i\}=\Sigma[(1^3 1)+\{1^{31}3\}]^n=\{\equiv\}$$

After bottling
out from taking
his own life like
Konrad Rudulf and
Johannes his elder
{br}Others {Ludwig}'s
poorly expressed
d-Act I conclusion
was that death is
not an event in LiFE
since we do not
sensually
experience iT
and that in body
full LiFE "Whereof
oNE cannot speak
thereof oNE must
pass by in
siLENCE"

siLENCE
smilefull
IV siLENCE
full d-aCT
faced sense
in d-eMPTY
to end there
fuLL d-Act III
iRONiC play
and land in
language
bODYFuLL
cLUELeSS
his mULeSS
break free of
enough to
he wasn't fly
investigations
philosophical
his d-Act II
Alas in

$$\{i\}=\Sigma[(1^31)+\{1^{31}3\}]^n=\{\equiv\}$$

d-aCT II's

d-aCT II's

$$\{i\}=\Sigma[(1^70)+\{1^31\}]^n=\{\overline{\overline{}}\}$$

dERRi{dA} unlike (QUiNE)
did not get iT His way of
philosophy involved the
b-littling d-littlement of
aLL of the Works of past
philosophical dADDY
{br}OTHERs There being
'nothing beyond their Texts'
Texts being simply chains of
suggestionless Signifiers that
lead neither up nor down but
siDEways iT's aLL in {h}is
brackets not in {h}is Texts!
there's 'nothing beyond'
remember! Little did he know
poor desperate little d-littling
Continental man There's lot's
lot's like {h}im over there
according to (QUiNE) aLL
floundering in expanses of
unregimented Signifiers aLL
of their own making

(QUiNE)
quantifying
iT identifying &
(hE) certainly got

talk of tHiNGs
such ontological
simply regiments all
1st Order LoGiC
for (him) whilst
phiLOLOGY"
recapitulates
"onTOLOGY
Logical talk
and higher ordering
and setting aside aLL 2nd
beyond! Despite deriding

logically be anything
So how could there
texts according to him
being nothing in {h}is
d-constructions there
dERRi{dA}'s unhinged
(QUiNE) raged & b-littled

$\{i\}=\Sigma[\{1^{31}3\}.(1^{4}04')]^{n}=(\equiv)$

d-aCT I's

d-aCT I's

$$\{i\}=\Sigma[(1^3 1)+\{1^{31}3\}]^n=\{\equiv\}$$

In the midst
of his [1/3] spin on
aDULTescent things
{hEiSENBERG} took a
d-eMPTY sensefull
mATRiX mechanical
approach in all things
Quantum probable
"Shut up and
calculate" his
response to
the tiny
little wave
particle
musings of
(scHRODiNGER)
& that oTHER
sTANDARD
cOPENHAGEN
modeling
[LoT]

neithers
'd-aCT IV'
nor there
and here
& there boths
'd-aCT III' here
superpositioned
'd-aCT II' theres
'd-aCT I' heres
wave function
collapse of their
how of the pointfull
the where, when and
their uncertainties of
totally bemused by
cOPENHAGEN [Lot]
functioning
That wave

$$[U]=[1^31]=[\rlap{=}{\equiv}]$$

d-aCT II's

d-aCT I's

$$\{i\}=\Sigma[\{1\,^604'\}^*(1\,^31)^*\{1\,^604'\}]^n=\{\equiv\}$$

And think @ how {Buddha)}
must have felt when he realised
his Hindu {br}Others and sisters
had not yet sussed that their
transcendental aTMAN was
simply a jIVA deluded not
like him j'anatmoi mih

acknowledge
analyse and
to desperately
a state that he needed
state of Kharmic Delusion
deeds that he persisted in his
a result of his past dare-devil
had taught him that iT was as
Hindu {br}Others and sisters
And think @ how his

$[U]=[1^7 0]=[⁝⁝]$

d-aCT II's

d-aCT I's

$$\{i\}=\Sigma[\{1^604'\}*(1^71)*\{1^604'\}]^n=\{\equiv\}$$

**Edmund 'full of
Western promise'
{Husserl)} in his
pHenomenoLogical
reductive take on things
intensionally bracketed off
his Eastern {br}Others first
5 sETs of sENSIBLEs plus their
6th of thought-ou tHiNGs
the vulgar's uMWeLT before
inflating their 7th into his
oNE and only transcendental
eGO tHiNG confined to conscious
awareness of spatio-temporal
sENSIBLEs understood in terms of
pre-formed intellectual iNTUiTiONs
that endlessly lead into choicefully
ordered transinfinite sets of Georgie
boY 'turtles' unfull fillable
Cantorian 'turtles' aLL the
way up that greatly satisfied
the incomplete (GödeL)**

analyse & drop
to desperately
state that he needed
of kharmic delusion a
he persisted in his state
thought-out tHiNG that
transcendental eGO
a result of his unbracketed
had taught him that iT was as
Buddhist {br}Others and sisters
his 'full of Eastern promise'
And think @ how

$$[U]=[1^70]=[\vdots\vdots]$$

d-aCT II's

d-aCT I's

$$\{i\}=\Sigma[(1^{7}0)+\{1^{7}0\}]^{n}=\{::\}$$

{hEGEL} in his
aDULTescent 'Logic"'
trivialized the excluded middle
of (aRiSTOTLE) by separating and
locating aLL of his contradictory
thesis's and anti-thesis's
diaLECTiCALLY driving
concrete historical
change within
differing historical
periods ended by
grounding iT aLL
absolutely in
a pure miRROR
Less state of
oTHERLess
bEiNG

sMiLiNGs
post mE-fuLL
oTHERiNGs and
in d-eMPTY fACEed
"PHENOMENOLOGY"
his oTHERfull
grounding
failed in
he mULessly
state however
post miRRORing
In his subsequent

$$\{i\}=\Sigma[(1^70)+\{1^70\}]^n=\{\text{⠿}\}$$

d-aCT ~~IV's~~

d-aCT I's

$$\{i\}=\Sigma[(1^70).\{1^704'\}]^n=\{\equiv\}$$

{zHU} a
philosophicaly
inclined well be
haved Chinese
man a Confucian
man gradually
thought of the
'LighTsome
fuLLness of iT
aLL' in terms
of immanent
(Qi) termed
complimentary
yiN & yANG stuFF
mE U & iT-like stuFF
'LighTsome' patterned
stuFF patterned aLL
by (Qi)'s patterning
partner {Li}

between
LighTsome in
the patterned
'fuLLness of
bordering the
and beYOND
of the bACK
eMPTYNESS
the utter
sittings of
in our own
U and mE with
different from
the thought no
instantly had the
fuLLness of iT aLL'
of the 'LighTsome
within his sittings
his confrontation
Buddhist mAN in
b-littling Indian
a b-littled logically
{nAGARJUNa}

$\{i\}=\Sigma[(1^{31}3).\{1^{4}04'\}]^{n}=\{\equiv\}$

d-aCT I's

d-aCT I's

$$(i)=\Sigma[(1^70)^*\{1^70\}]^n=\{\text{▤}\}$$

(Emily} was a
{no}BODY Just
like U and
[m]E How
dreary to be a
[some]BODY
How Public
like a Frog
to tell one's
name the live
long day to an
unadmiring
sOD!

bOG!
admiring
long day to an

name the live
to tell one's
like a Frog
How Public
[some]bODY
dreary to be a
you know! How
They'd advertise
of U Don't tell
Then there's a pair
a [no]BODY too?
are yoU? Are yoU
a [no]BODY Who
{Marilyn} was a
Sometimes

$$(i)=\Sigma[(1^70).\{1^704'\}]^n=\{\equiv\}$$

d-aCT II's

ShOWiNG nEXT

Printed in Great Britain
by Amazon

66393515R10163